ERS

What We Know About:

Effective Classroom Management to Support Student Learning

Educational Research Service

Because research and information make the difference.

Educational Research Service
2000 Clarendon Boulevard, Arlington, VA 22201-2908
Tel: (703) 243-2100 or (800) 791-9308
Fax: (703) 243-1985 or (800) 791-9309
Email: ers@ers.org • Web site: www.ers.org

Educational Research Service is the nonprofit organization serving the research and information needs of the nation's K-12 education leaders and the public. Founded by seven national school management associations, ERS provides quality, objective research and information that enable local school district administrators to make the most effective school decisions, both in terms of day-to-day operations and long-range planning. Refer to the last page of this publication to learn how you can benefit from the services and resources available through an annual ERS Subscription.

ERS offers a number of research-based resources that particularly complement this report on the teaching of reading. Please refer to the Order Form at the back of this publication for a listing of some of these materials. Alternatively, visit us online at www.ers.org for a more complete overview of the wealth of K-12 research and information products and services available through ERS.

ERS Founding Organizations:
American Association of School Administrators
American Association of School Personnel Administrators
Association of School Business Officials International
Council of Chief State School Officers
National Association of Elementary School Principals
National Association of Secondary School Principals
National School Public Relations Association

Ordering information: Additional copies of *Effective Classroom Management to Support Student Learning* may be purchased at the base price of $22 each (ERS School District Subscriber price: $11; ERS Individual Subscriber price: $16.50). Quantity discounts available. Stock No. 0628. ISBN 1-931762-34-1.

Order from: Educational Research Service, 2000 Clarendon Boulevard, Arlington, VA 22201-2908. Telephone: (800) 791-9308. Fax: (800) 791-9309. Email: ers@ers.org. Web site: www.ers.org. Add the greater of $4.50 or 10% of total purchase price for postage and handling. Phone orders accepted with Visa, MasterCard, or American Express.

ERS Management Staff:
John M. Forsyth, Ph.D., President and Director of Research
Katherine A. Behrens, Senior Director of Marketing and Member Services

Authors: Elizabeth Shellard, senior research specialist with Nancy Protheroe, director of special research projects and Jennifer Turner, research specialist.

Note: ERS is solely responsible for this publication; no approval or endorsement by ERS founders is implied.

© 2005, Educational Research Service. All Rights Reserved.

Contents

Foreword v

Chapter 1
   Introduction 1

Chapter 2
   **The Link between Classroom Management
   and Student Learning** 3
      Elements of Effective Classroom Management 4
      Teaching about Appropriate Student Behavior 8

Chapter 3
   Key Elements of Effective Classroom Management 11
      Using a Prevention-Oriented Approach 11
      Keeping Discipline Positive 16
      Instructional Strategies that Support Classroom Management 19
         Using Time Efficiently 19
         Paying Attention to the Physical Layout of the Classroom 23
         Providing Instruction Matched to Students' Needs and Abilities 23
         Providing Instruction in Ways Students Find Interesting 24
         Moving through the Classroom as You Teach 26
         Providing Students with Success Experiences 28
      Some Special Issues for Today's Classrooms 29

Chapter 4
   Promoting Student Self-Management 35
      Establishing Guidelines for Acceptable Behavior 36
         The Role of "Rules" 36
         Student Participation in the Development of Rules 37
      Additional Ways to Promote the Development of Student
      Self-Management Skills 38
         Involving Students in "Running" the Classroom 38
         Teaching Conflict Resolution Skills 41
         Working with Individual Students 43

Chapter 5
Dealing with Problem Behaviors 47
    Expectations, Caring, and Consistency 48
    Taking a Proactive Approach 49
    Dealing with Challenging Behaviors 50
    Looking for "Triggers" to Misbehavior 52
    Taking a Strategic Approach to Misbehavior 56
    Dealing with More Serious Behavior Problems 58
    Ineffective Disciplinary Practices 64
    Working with Parents to Improve Student Behavior 66

Chapter 6
A Schoolwide Approach to Behavior Management and Discipline 67
    Elements of an Effective Schoolwide Approach 69
        Consistency Is Key 73
    Developing a Schoolwide Discipline Plan 74
    Avoiding the "Traps" 77
    Communicating the Plan 78
    What Some Schools Have Done 78
    The Role of the Principal 81

Chapter 7
Concluding Remarks 85

References 89

Foreword

Today's high-stakes environment in schools makes it critical that every minute count toward ensuring students achieve at high levels. Thus, today—perhaps more than ever before—classroom management issues are important to frontline educators.

It makes intuitive sense that teaching and learning can progress more smoothly and productively in a classroom characterized by on-task and nondisruptive student behavior. However, less than one of every five first-year teachers responding to a U.S. Department of Education survey considered themselves to be "very well prepared" to handle a range of classroom management and discipline situations. And the problems are not limited to new teachers. Three of every 10 teachers responding to a Public Agenda survey agreed with the survey item "Too many teachers are ineffective at classroom management."

The authors of this *What We Know About* characterize an effective teacher's approach to classroom management as maintaining a "delicate balance of control, while not stifling students' energy and creativity." This balance requires high levels of teacher knowledge and skills.

Effective Classroom Management to Support Student Learning was developed as a teacher resource on this complex topic. The publication blends research findings, informed opinions from the professional literature, and experience about what constitutes best practice to address a variety of important issues. It is intended to help new teachers as they develop important skills—and to assist experienced teachers as they work to expand their repertoire of strategies.

This *What We Know About* also recognizes and discusses the importance of a schoolwide aproach to promoting good behavior. In schools where principals, teachers, and other staff work together to develop rules, consequences for breaking these rules, and ways to recognize good behavior—and then apply these consistently—it is more likely that the school culture will be one that focuses on teaching and learning.

We hope this ERS resource supports classroom teachers as well as the education leaders working with them in their efforts to develop well-managed, learning-centered classrooms.

John M. Forsyth
President and Director of Research

Chapter 1

Introduction

Most teachers-in-training remember their own days in elementary, middle, or high school and the students who sometimes disrupted class. But—even as their teacher preparation classes highlight the importance of effective classroom management techniques—these teachers-to-be most likely remain focused on the instructional aspects of teaching.

It is not until they begin teaching that they realize the connection between the classroom environment and teaching and learning. When asked, both new and experienced teachers agree "in overwhelming numbers that good student behavior is . . . an essential condition before teaching and learning can take place" (Public Agenda 2004, 8). Learning how to "manage" their classrooms, however, is one of the most difficult aspects of the job for many teachers.

A key to effective classroom management is understanding instruction and management are not separate tasks but are inextricably related (Wilson 1996). For example, a well-planned, well-paced, and interesting lesson aligned with student abilities and needs engages students and so decreases the likelihood that student misbehavior will occur. And learning is likely to occur at higher levels in well-managed classrooms in which disruption is an exception, not the rule.

This view of the link between classroom management and instruction also fits well with the realities of group dynamics present in every classroom. One Florida teacher characterizes the typical classroom as including a small group of students who are typically "eager and ready to learn," another small group of students who are more likely to "make trouble or act the class clown," and a large group of students who act as the:

> "swing vote," those students who follow the prevailing atmosphere.... In essence, when a teacher enforces the rules, deals effectively with the tougher cases and insists on accountability, students quickly learn what is and is not permissible and behave accordingly (Public Agenda 2004, 18).

Thus, an important aspect of a teacher's role is to act in ways that reinforce good behavior—and discourage inappropriate behavior—by this group of swing-vote students.

Willis suggests teachers are less likely to be successful if they rely on the "old" view of classroom management focused primarily on discipline. Most educators now agree "authoritarian approaches may get students to comply, but they don't help students develop discipline and responsibility" (1996, 1).

Thus, the most successful classroom managers are constantly—and often almost automatically—engaged in a complex set of behaviors that keep learning on track. This *What We Know About* highlights some key aspects of those behaviors, including:

- the link between instruction and management;
- development of the daily routines and structures that contribute to a smoothly run classroom—and so to high levels of student learning;
- efforts to build students' ability to manage their own behavior;
- strategies for dealing effectively with problem behaviors; and
- the role teacher attitudes and behaviors play in establishing a learning-focused classroom.

In addition, the publication includes a discussion of the key role a schoolwide approach to behavior management can play in establishing an environment that supports appropriate behavior and discourages misbehavior. By working together, principals, teachers, and other school staff are more likely to develop a school culture focused on learning.

Chapter 2

The Link between Classroom Management and Student Learning

The job of a teacher is first and foremost to instruct, not simply to "manage." Yet management and instruction are inherently interdependent—in order for the learning environment to be its best, both elements must be present and working side by side, all the time.

Good management supports the ability to provide good instruction. If students are aware of rules and procedures, if materials and equipment are organized, and if the teacher deals with disruption quickly, instruction will flow more smoothly, and students can focus on the lesson at hand. Just as important, good instruction supports development of an orderly classroom. When lessons are well planned, objectives are clear, and learning is meaningful, discipline problems occur less frequently. Students are on task and interested in what they are learning, and they have less reason to be disruptive.

Porch and Protheroe describe effective classroom management as:

> proactive by nature; it not only addresses current discipline problems . . . it keeps future problems from occurring.... A teacher in a well-managed classroom has a plan, a structure, and guidelines that are communicated to and understood by *all* students, and that plan recognizes that different types of behavior may be appropriate for the variety of instructional approaches used in today's schools. The bottom line is the maintenance of an atmosphere in which students can learn, an environment that is both intellectually stimulating and physically and emotionally safe (2002, 1-2).

The American Federation of Teachers highlights the importance of good teaching to creating and maintaining a classroom in which good student behavior is the norm:

A teacher who has mastered classroom management skills keeps students constructively engaged and learning from the moment they enter the room. A good classroom manager carefully plans everything that occurs in the classroom, from the seating arrangement to instructions for children who finish planned activities early.

To the untrained eye, this teacher's classroom management skills may appear to be more art than science, leaving the impression that effective classroom management is instinctive rather than a learned craft. Effective classroom management, however, can be taught. With time and effort, teachers can become more effective classroom managers.

The heart of effective classroom management rests on ensuring that the instructional techniques, classroom arrangement, and classroom rules and procedures are all well thought out and supportive of the instructional program and students' learning. Instructional techniques will vary widely, depending on the material being taught and the age and ability of the students.... While there may be limitations on the physical arrangement of a classroom, the most effective classroom managers have arranged their rooms to minimize disruptions and support instructional techniques (n.d., 5).

"To the untrained eye, this teacher's classroom management skills may appear to be more art than science" (American Federation of Teachers n.d., 5).

Elements of Effective Classroom Management

Research conducted in a wide variety of situations has identified critical components of effective classroom management. Highlights from several of these studies make clear the importance of good instructional strategies to maintaining an environment focused on teaching and learning.

Wang, Haertel, and Walberg (1993/1994) analyzed a knowledge base representing 11,000 statistical findings connecting a variety of variables with student achievement in order to answer the question: what helps students learn? Twenty-eight categories of factors, classified into six broad types of influences—

such as student aptitude, classroom instruction and climate, and school organization—were rated as to their relative positive impact on learning.

Of the 28 categories, classroom management ranked first, with a "score" of 64.8, just ahead of student metacognitive process (63.0) and cognitive processes (61.3). In the researchers' view, "effective classroom management increases student engagement, decreases disruptive behaviors, and makes good use of instructional time" (1993/1994, 76). Their definition of effective classroom management included a variety of instructional elements such as effective questioning/recitation strategies, learner accountability, smooth transitions—as well as teacher "with-it-ness."

> **"Effective classroom management increases student engagement, decreases disruptive behaviors, and makes good use of instructional time" (Wang, Haertel, and Walberg 1993/1994, 76).**

This last skill—"with-it-ness"—was further detailed in a study conducted by Morrow et al. and designed to answer the question: "what is the nature of exemplary early literacy instruction?" They found that exemplary teachers:

> . . . were extremely aware of what was happening in their rooms. They were virtually always in a position where they could see everyone in the room . . . [they] seemed extremely attuned to intervening before a problem escalated in the classroom. Like good parents, these teachers seemed to possess a sixth sense for when things became too noisy, or even too quiet, in an area of the classroom. The high level of with-it-ness was a prominent element of the exemplary teachers' classroom management style (1999, 470).

Morrow et al. described other characteristics of effective classroom management leading to high student achievement:

> Teachers were consistent in their management techniques, so children knew what was expected of them and consequently carried out work that needed to be done. The day flowed smoothly from one activity to another, and routines were regular. The activities were varied to keep the children engaged. Furthermore, the affective quality in the rooms was exemplary;

teachers were warm and caring.... In such an atmosphere, children learned to respect the teacher and one another (1999, 474).

Taylor et al. observed 104 kindergarten through third-grade teachers and then categorized them as "most accomplished," "moderately accomplished," and "least accomplished" based on the degree to which they demonstrated elements of effective instruction. The "most accomplished" teachers:

> were experts at classroom management.... In general, they had well-established classroom routines and procedures for handling behavior problems, quick transitions between activities, and a rapid pace of instruction, thus allowing for high instructional density. [They] managed, on average, to engage virtually all (96%) of their students in the work of the classroom (1999, 44).

In contrast, the on-task rate for moderately accomplished teachers was 84 percent, and the rate for the least accomplished teachers was 61 percent.

> "In our careers as elementary and secondary school teachers and principals, we consistently saw instructional quality and effective management of student behavior as complementary. Effective teachers experienced the fewest in-class student behavior problems, probably because they were: (a) well informed in their subjects; (b) well informed about their students; (c) professionally careful in their selection of their behaviors; (d) in possession of a rich instructional repertoire; and (e) fundamentally interesting people. In short, our experience suggests that a powerful way of preventing discipline problems lies in improving lesson planning and delivery" (Hartzell and Petrie 1992, 377).

Several other studies identified aspects of good classroom management as being strongly linked to higher levels of student learning:

- The classroom management system emphasizes curriculum-related activities and maintaining student engagement in those activities (Brophy n.d., 10). The teacher does not see discipline as a separate issue or as a "set of controls." Faced with a problem, such teachers "find something the student is interested in, find something else the student can do, find something else the student can share." In other words, these teachers "view discipline primarily as a natural consequence of their ability to interest and involve learners" (Haberman 1995, 5-6).

- The teacher is consistently well prepared and follows predictable, although not rigid, patterns of behavior and activities. Students know

---

Research-Based Classroom Management Strategies

Drawing from more than 100 research reports, Marzano, Marzano, and Pickering (2003) describe four fundamental factors that work to create effective classroom management:

- *Rules and procedures.* Although rules may differ from teacher to teacher, the authors identify basic areas of classroom operations that should be addressed—general classroom behavior, beginning and ending of the school day or period, transitions and interruptions, use of materials and equipment, group work, and seatwork and teacher-led activities.

- *Disciplinary interventions.* Research supports striking a balance between negative consequences for bad behavior and positive consequences for good behavior.

- *Teacher-student relationships.* A positive teacher-student relationship can help encourage students to follow rules and accept discipline. The teacher should let students know who is in charge. However, teachers should temper this by ensuring students of their interest in them both individually and as a class.

- *Mental set.* Effective classroom managers undertake their duties with a specific "mental set," or frame of mind. Capable leaders display both "with-it-ness" and emotional objectivity. With-it-ness is an awareness of student behavior and the ability to recognize and immediately address potential problems. Emotional objectivity refers to the capacity to conduct a businesslike relationship with students, even though strong feelings might be involved.

what is expected of them (Wharton-McDonald, Pressley, and Hampston 1998).

- The teacher minimizes disruptive behavior by redirecting students in a positive way before the problem becomes overt (Wharton-McDonald, Pressley, and Hampston 1998).

A U.S. Department of Education study described one "highly effective" teacher's management style as:

> . . . calm and quiet. She is remarkably effective at maintaining order despite the fact that the classroom is one of four clustered together in a semi-open pod arrangement. She uses a combination of quiet reminders and individual praise for So-and-So, who is sitting nicely now. The result is that students do what she asks the first time she asks, with rare exceptions (which are quickly brought into line), and attention is not drawn to management issues very often. The children devote nearly all of their energy to academic tasks and other aspects of the school's curriculum (Knapp, Shields, and Turnbull 1992, 12).

Finally, in a study of 26 high-achieving, high-poverty schools in Texas, researchers found students in successful classrooms were more likely to be actively engaged in learning on a daily basis—and so less likely to engage in off-task and disruptive behavior. The researchers discuss this:

> The focus on the academic success of every student was evident in the planning of individual teachers.... Teachers planned lessons with a focus on getting each and every student to succeed academically. Teachers were attuned to the special ways in which individual students learned best. They exploited this knowledge to create learning environments that allowed many students to attain challenging academic skills (Lein, Johnson, and Ragland 1997, 5).

Teaching about Appropriate Student Behavior

There is another link between instruction and classroom management. Especially in the early grades, children need to be instructed on classroom rules and procedures through modeling and practice. In addition, many students may need to be explicitly taught about good behavior. Cotton talks about this:

Effective management . . . is more an instructional than a disciplinary enterprise. Effective managers socialize their students to the student role through instruction and modeling. It is important that these teachers are consistent in articulating demands and monitoring compliance, but the most important thing is to make sure that students know what to do in the first place (2001, online).

Cotton identified specific attitudes and behaviors of teachers that support the development of acceptable student behavior. These include:

- *Holding and communicating high expectations for student learning and behavior.* Through the personal warmth and encouragement they express to students and the classroom requirements they establish, effective teachers make sure that students know they are expected to learn well and behave appropriately.

- *Establishing and clearly teaching classroom rules and procedures.* Effective teachers teach behavioral rules and classroom routines in much the same way as they teach instructional content, and they review these frequently at the beginning of the school year and periodically thereafter. Classroom rules are posted in classrooms.

- *Specifying consequences and their relation to student behavior.* Effective teachers are careful to explain the connection between students' misbehavior and teacher-imposed sanctions. This connection, too, is taught and reviewed as needed.

- *Enforcing classroom rules promptly, consistently, and equitably.* Effective teachers respond quickly to misbehavior, respond in the same way at different times, and impose consistent sanctions regardless of the gender, race, or other personal characteristics of misbehaving students.

- *Sharing with students the responsibility for classroom management.* Effective teachers work to inculcate in students a sense of belonging and self-discipline, rather than viewing discipline as something imposed from the outside.

- *Maintaining a brisk pace for instruction and making smooth transitions between activities.* Effective teachers keep things moving in their classrooms, which increases learning as well as reduces the likelihood of misbehavior.

- *Monitoring classroom activities and providing feedback and reinforcement.* Effective teachers observe and comment on student behavior, and they reinforce appropriate behavior through the provision of verbal, symbolic, and tangible rewards (2001, online).

Chapter 3

Key Elements of Effective Classroom Management

Effective classroom management already has been described as requiring a complex set of teacher knowledge and skills. In addition, the link between instruction and classroom management has been briefly discussed. This chapter provides an overview of specific approaches teachers can use as part of their classroom management "portfolio." Although many of the approaches are more typically classified as instructional techniques, they also support effective classroom management because they keep students actively engaged in learning.

Using a Prevention-Oriented Approach

As with so many aspects of a teacher's role, attitudes play a significant part in developing a classroom environment in which problem behavior happens infrequently. A classic overview of research conducted by Good (1987) demonstrated a connection between teacher expectations and student achievement. An intervening variable was teacher behavior toward individual students. For example, teachers were observed to praise students for whom they have low expectations less frequently, interact with them less frequently, allow them less time to respond to questions before redirecting unanswered questions to other class members, and provide briefer and less informative feedback to the questions of low achievers.

Research also has shown that teachers' expectations for students tend to be self-fulfilling. That is, students tend to give to teachers as much or as little as teachers expect of them (Lumsden 1997). And from their first years in school, students are able to perceive differences in teachers' expectations for their own performance and that of their peers (Gottfredson et al. 1995). On a more positive note, when teachers maintain high expectations, they encourage in students a desire to aim high rather than slide by (Lumsden 1997).

Teacher expectations can have a similar relationship with student behavior. For example, Mills and Bulach (1996) found that teachers who developed a well-thought-out discipline plan that emphasized positive expectations for behavior had fewer behavior problems. This makes intuitive sense. Most teachers have heard at least one student say: "everyone expects me to be a problem so what's the use of trying?" Contrast this with a student whose teacher communicates an expectation of good behavior—and supports this expectation with reasonable rules that are consistently applied.

Other aspects of taking a prevention-oriented approach are more concrete. Proactive, prevention-oriented approaches are successful because they make expectations clear and decrease the likelihood students will misbehave because they misunderstand the boundaries between acceptable and unacceptable behavior.

For example, Wong and Wong (1998) talk about the importance of the first day of school in establishing the tenor of a classroom. In particular, they stress the need to implement routines on the first day that will be used for the rest of the year.

The Collaborative for Excellence in Teacher Preparation talks briefly about some of these routines:

> Establishing clear expectations for student behavior is the primary purpose for setting up classroom routines. If students are familiar with the processes necessary to get a particular job done, they are more likely to complete it in an orderly manner. Develop plans for these activities that work for your physical space and your management style. If a routine is not effective, you can involve your students in redesigning the routine.
>
> - *Movement.* Develop plans for entering and exiting the classroom and changing class configurations, such as moving from whole class to small-group instruction. Also plan for movement of individual students to meet needs such as pencil sharpening and getting personal supplies.
>
> - *Materials management.* If routines are developed for the distribution, collection, and storage of instructional materials, student helpers will be able to complete them quickly.

- *Transitions.* If instructional materials are prepared and organized, transitions between activities will be smooth and take little time. Necessary materials might be listed on the daily schedule so students will know what they need and can prepare for one activity as materials for the previous activity are stored or collected.

- *Group work.* Each team member within a group should have a job, and over time each student should have an opportunity to do each job. Develop job descriptions and routines for assigning the jobs. Jobs might be facilitator, time-keeper, reporter, recorder, encourager, questioner, materials manager, taskmaster—make up your own or use one of the many plans that have been developed (n.d., online).

Although classroom rules were briefly mentioned in a previous section, they should be discussed again as an aspect of a proactive approach to classroom management. A *Teaching Today* article provides some helpful suggestions related to developing, communicating, and applying rules:

- *Familiarize yourself with the school rules and procedures related to discipline.* For example, make sure you have a clear understanding of when your principal or assistant principal wants to be involved with behavior problems.

- *Prepare a brief list of general expectations for student behavior in your classroom.* As you do this, keep in mind both school rules and the type of environment you wish to establish in your classroom.

- *Develop a brief list of actual "rules" for your classroom*—as well as consequences for infractions.

- *Discuss both the rules and consequences with your students—and apply these consistently, especially during the first few weeks of school.* Just as important during the beginning weeks is the consistent use of praise and other rewards for good behavior (n.d., online).

Effective Classroom Management to Support Student Learning

Preventing Behavior Problems: What Works

Positive consequences matter: Provide positive consequences to increase desirable behaviors.

Research findings: One of the best-established principles of learning is that appropriate, immediate positive consequences can make the behavior more frequent. This process is commonly called positive reinforcement. Similarly, increasing positive incentives for alternatives to problem behavior can lead to decreases in problem behavior.

In Schools:

- Teachers should provide positive consequences for positive social as well as academic accomplishments, particularly with children and youth that misbehave frequently.

- Consequences can come in many forms: positive attention, praise, privileges, access to desirable activities, prizes and money all act as positive consequences. Children showing problem behavior may need more frequent, immediate and salient positive consequences to improve their behavior than children with fewer problems. All children, however, can benefit from knowing when they have done a good job, either academically or socially.

- Teachers with large numbers of children who misbehave should examine whether adults or other children are unknowingly providing positive consequences—particularly attention—for the behavior they want to discourage. Rearranging the environment so that children get attention, privileges, etc., for more positive social and academic behavior can help this situation.

Effective negative consequences matter: Clear, immediate, mild negative consequences can reduce problem behaviors.

Research findings: Just as positive consequences can increase the chances a behavior will occur, effective negative consequences will reduce its probability…. Behavior often decreases when that behavior "costs" the person something in time, money or undesirable consequences. The reason punishment often fails to work is probably because the punishment is too severe, too delayed and too inconsistent. Costs and other negative consequences will work best if: (a) negative consequences or costs occur immediately after the behavior; (b) negative consequences are consistent rather than occasional; and (c) the child receives positive consequences for desirable alternative behaviors. Gradually increasing the intensity of punishment is not effective in the long run, either. Instead, relatively mild negative consequences delivered consistently are more likely to be effective—particularly when expectations for acceptable behavior are clear.

In Schools:

- Teachers should communicate classroom rules clearly so children understand which behaviors will result in negative consequences.

- Teachers and parents should provide brief, immediate, mild and consistent negative consequences for problem behavior. Examples include short, private reprimands that label the problem behavior clearly; brief loss of privileges; or brief isolation from an activity the child enjoys.

- Teachers' negative consequences will work best if teachers also establish warm, positive relationships with their students and if they provide positive consequences for pro-social alternatives to problem behaviors.

- Teachers and adults should avoid negative consequences that have the potential to harm the child either physically or psychologically (e.g. insulting children publicly).

- Teachers and other adults should carefully keep track of problems to see if their negative consequences decrease the frequency of problem behaviors. If not, they should try alternative ways of handling the child's behavior (excerpted from Foster et al. 2002, 10-13).

Keeping Discipline Positive

Lindberg, Kelley, and Swick discuss developing whole-class reward systems that may be more effective than negative consequences for breaking rules. In their view, such approaches can both "encourage the appropriate behavior of the challenging students . . . [and] recognize the others for not reinforcing inappropriate behavior" (2005, 36). They go on to provide some specific suggestions:

- Be consistent. If you bend the rules on a regular basis or only enforce them once things get out of hand, your students will roll the dice to see if today is the day they may be lucky and not get into trouble for their behavior.

- Focus on the positive. Rather than take things away, allow students to work toward earning something.

- Set a behavioral goal that can be attained in a reasonable time frame. If you set a goal that is nearly impossible to meet, or if the incentive attached is too far in the distance, students may lose interest.

- Avoid an all-or-nothing approach. Provide ways to earn incremental rewards. Students—especially those whose behavior is challenging—won't be interested in earning rewards if they seem impossible for them to attain. Remember, the objective of the management system is to teach students how to behave in your classroom—they need consistent and ongoing encouragement (2005, 36).

Nina Shandler, an educational psychologist, advocates using positive discipline methods for dealing with students with challenging behaviors and, more generally, for effective classroom management. She provides the following account of her interactions with an especially challenging student:

> Jake taught me to use a magical question—a question basic to positive discipline—"What did you do right?" Jake had been in our school, and in trouble, since first grade. Kindhearted and exuberant, he would begin with misdemeanors. Once corrected, however, Jake went from committing minor offenses to classroom felonies. He argued, he screamed, he stomped his feet, he threw things.
>
> By the time I began working with him, Jake was in fourth grade and he was infamous. He routinely spent entire days in the vice

principal's office. Both teachers and students expected Jake to interfere with learning. They showed little tolerance for even inconsequential acts of noncompliance when Jake was the culprit. But for the first couple of months, my relationship with Jake was fresh, unspoiled by insults or accusations.

Then one morning I saw Jake and his best friend running down the hall full tilt, scattering frightened first-graders in their wake. I stood between the two boys and the playground door. I uttered two words, "Please walk." Jake's friend skidded to a halt, said "Sorry" and proceeded slowly out the door.

Jake stopped, stood directly in front of me and screamed, "I wasn't running! You're not fair. You tricked me. You don't even like me. I never want to talk to you, ever again!"

I responded, "We really do need to talk. Let's go to my office." I turned and walked toward the office, motioning for him to follow. He walked behind me, more in pursuit than in obedience, pointing at me and loudly announcing to the children in the hall, "I hate that stupid teacher!"

When we arrived in my office, I sat down. Jake paced as he boisterously lamented his fate: "You're all alike—all you teachers. All you do is catch me doing things wrong. Why doesn't anybody ask me what I do right for a change?"

His request seemed reasonable. I set aside my irritation, composed myself and asked, "What did you do right today?"

Surprised, he answered, "I didn't do anything right today. You saw me. I ran down the hall. I refused to walk. I yelled at you. I did everything wrong!"

I contradicted him. "You came with me. You could have refused, but you didn't. Thank you."

Jake sat down, silent. I was feeding him a message he craved to hear. "When I asked you what you did right, you told me what you did wrong. You took responsibility. I know it's hard for you to take responsibility, but you did it. I think you can be proud of yourself."

By now Jake was calm and quiet, listening carefully. After a moment, he said, "Sorry. I don't really hate you."

That conversation gave Jake and me a foundation for working on his overreactions. I didn't have to force confessions or apologies. I asked him about his positive behavior. When necessary, I helped him remember good things he had done. Feeling affirmed, he found the strength to take responsibility and mend relationships. Teachers and students alike welcomed him back to class.

The simple question Jake taught me—"What did you do right?"—has proven the most versatile tool in my positive discipline tool kit. It works magic, building personal responsibility and repairing damaged self-esteem (1996, online).

Shandler acknowledges using positive reinforcement approaches sometimes requires enormous self-discipline when facing behavior such as that described above. In her view, however, the long-term benefits are clear. Her discipline "tool kit" is briefly described below:

- *Define a goal.* Look toward the long term. What's important for students to know and value? Self-respect? Empathy? Responsibility? Cooperation? Consideration? Tolerance? Keep this goal in mind.

- *Recognize positive steps.* What behaviors, feelings, attitudes or skills move students toward that goal? Accepting compliments and corrections? Asserting their needs? Concentrating on their work? Appreciating another viewpoint? Understanding the effects of their behavior? Listening? Sharing? Practice recognizing these attitudes and actions.

- *Reinforce positives.* Reinforce even the smallest steps forward. Help students notice their accomplishments and appreciate the accomplishments of others by offering praise, applause, tickets, and other rewards when appropriate.

- *Disarm negatives.* What can be done about the negative behaviors and attitudes that impede progress? Do what's needed to take away their power: ignore, change the focus, offer positive alternatives. Never give negative behavior status by publicly reprimanding or by writing names on the blackboard or by engaging in an argument.

- *Appreciate progress.* How can you maintain optimism? Measure progress often, remember where you began, and appreciate every step forward (excerpted from Shandler 1996, online).

Finally, Kay and Ryan (2000) suggest that actually teaching social skills can contribute to efforts to keep discipline positive.

Instructional Strategies that Support Classroom Management

A brief discussion earlier in this *What We Know About* described instruction and management as inherently interdependent. Effective classroom managers recognize this mutually dependent relationship and incorporate both instructional and managerial strategies into their approaches for promoting a good learning environment. Effective management strategies tend to have a common characteristic: they aim to heighten student engagement with learning, thus decreasing the likelihood of problem behavior while promoting higher levels of student learning.

In the view of McLeod, Fisher, and Hoover, "three key elements stand out as critical components of a well-managed classroom" (2003, vi):

- efficient use of time and classroom space;
- use of strategies that influence students to make good choices—as contrasted with ones that attempt to control student behavior; and
- implementation of effective instructional strategies.

In this section of the book, some instructional strategies that support both learning and good behavior are briefly highlighted.

Using Time Efficiently

An important teacher skill that has been linked to high levels of student learning is the effective and efficient use of instructional time. Quality and pacing of instruction is one way teachers make efficient use of time. In their review of research focusing on teacher behavior and student achievement, Brophy and Good state that "the most consistently replicated findings link achievement to the quality and pacing of instruction" (1986, 360).

The relationship between classroom management and student engagement time also is well documented. Researchers have found that one of the hardest tasks teachers face is keeping students focused on a lesson for a sustained period of time. Engagement rates have been found to depend on the teacher's ability to organize and manage the classroom as an efficient learning environment where academic activities run smoothly, transitions are brief and orderly, and little time is spent getting organized or dealing with inattention or resistance.

Time on the Sofa: Recognizing and Encouraging Positive Behaviors

Mary Hendra, a high school social studies teacher, explains her use of the "Friday Sofa Award" to reward and encourage a wide range of positive behaviors in her classroom. In a commentary published in *The Christian Science Monitor*, she describes her use of certificates that award "sofa time" for good behavior:

> Another teacher had left a sofa in my room, which she could no longer use. Students gravitated to it during breaks, so it was a natural outgrowth to use the sofa as a "reward."
>
> Recipients weren't excused from work—I kept a clipboard nearby—but they did get to work from the comfort of the sofa. While sitting on it was enthusiastically received, I was surprised to see greater impact from the certificates.
>
> Long after students' day on the sofa, their certificates still adorned their notebooks and parents told me how much that award had meant to their child. Giving the sofa award seemed to keep some students motivated who might otherwise have put less effort toward the class....
>
> One student likened my award-giving speeches to the Academy Awards. My favorite part was talking about the great work done as I gave each recipient a personalized, signed certificate.
>
> Students don't have to be getting As to be doing great work. Throughout the semester, I recognized students at all grade levels. Good work starts with small actions—being willing to ask for help, finding out what they missed when they were absent, not giving up when presented a challenge. Students need to know these actions are valued.
>
> Not all students do them, nor do all even know which actions or skills will help them succeed academically and professionally. The Friday Sofa Award highlighted valuable skills and encouraged students to practice them.

Sometimes positive behaviors were so obvious, I couldn't not acknowledge them—facile use of technology to enhance a project, composing a music score as part of an in-class assignment, embracing their character in a role play.

Other times I sought the less visible skills that students express—improved note taking, planning ahead, asking thought-provoking questions.

"Today's recipient, even though she does not yet have the grade she wants in this class, has turned around her attitude toward the class and the work, and as a result has begun turning in higher quality work."

Within two or three weeks of starting the awards, the class had forgiven the "cheesy" aspect of the whole thing and applauded heartily for every recipient. They also looked for good work from their peers and themselves and brought my attention to work worthy of an award.

On anonymous course evaluations at the end of the school year, 73 percent said the Friday Sofa Award contributed to a more positive climate and 64 percent said it helped them identify skills for success....

In the class with the lowest skill levels, 80 percent said the Friday Sofa Award made some positive difference in class climate and 85 percent said it helped them identify skills for success.

"I believe our society doesn't spend enough time praising what is going well." This was part of my explanation when I first introduced the Friday Sofa Award to my students. There is absolutely a place for critical thought. I hold high expectations for all students in my class. In fact, my students often say I am the most demanding teacher they have ever had in high school.

If I am going to push them that hard, I have all the more responsibility to look for and praise their achievements along the way—whether small or large. And think about it—don't we all relish having our achievements recognized and applauded? (excerpted from Hendra 2004, online).

Some teachers begin every class period with a task for students to complete when they enter the room. Doing so starts the class on a productive note and emphasizes that classroom time is too valuable to waste. The beginning-of-class activity could be journal writing in response to a question or topic on the blackboard, writing in a personal journal, reading a book, or checking another student's work. Tasks that call for independent student work also allow teachers time to do short administrative tasks such as taking attendance or returning graded work (DiGiulio 1995).

For this strategy to be successful, however, teachers must take the time to teach students the routine, create opportunities for them to practice it, and provide feedback designed to help students continuously improve their ability to work independently. Students need to know it is expected they will enter the classroom and begin work immediately. Consistency is key, especially as students learn the routine, and everyday tasks need to be simple enough that they can be completed without assistance.

Effective lesson planning also contributes to a smooth flow of instruction. Seeman identifies three aspects of lessons that keep students focused on learning:

- *A perceived sense of order.* If students do not have an understanding of where the lesson has been or is heading, they become frustrated and lose their engagement with the learning process, and disruptions become more likely. Teachers can address this need before beginning the lesson by giving an overview, as well as during the lesson by periodically reviewing what has been covered and where the lesson is going.

- *Meaning and purpose.* One way to bring meaning to a lesson is to ask students to make connections between the lesson and their own knowledge or experiences.

- *A sense of momentum.* Teachers should keep the lesson moving, and be alert to students' levels of interest and attention (1988, 140).

Lindberg, Kelley, and Swick (2005) talk about the importance of developing and using methods to transition that make effective use of time and provide few opportunities for students to misbehave. These transitions may include entering the classroom—or leaving it, as well as transitioning from one instructional activity to another. They suggest making the procedures for these transitions clear to students and then using the procedures consistently.

Key Elements of Effective Classroom Management

Paying Attention to the Physical Layout of the Classroom

The physical environment of the classroom is an important factor in preventing behavior problems. To minimize distractions, the teacher might designate places in the classroom for specific activities—such as large-group instruction, individual student work, and timeout—or might redesign high-traffic areas to minimize congestion (Stewart, Evans, and Kaczynski 1997).

Seating arrangements should allow for clear lines of sight so teachers can easily monitor students in all parts of the room, and students can see presentation areas with minimal movement of chairs or desks. If feasible, students should face away from possible sources of distraction such as windows, hallways, and small-group work areas. Smith and Misra (1992) suggest seating typically engaged students throughout the room to serve as models for other students.

Providing Instruction Matched to Students' Needs and Abilities

Teachers in well-managed classrooms recognize students are individuals who have individual needs and preferences. Like teachers—who have preferred instructional styles—different students learn best in different ways.

"Ask not how smart is the child, but how is the child smart?" (Howard Gardner in Sousa 2003, 35).

O'Neil talks about important teacher behaviors related to learning styles:

> Expert teachers have always accommodated students' individual differences . . . by explaining new concepts several ways or giving students several options for demonstrating mastery. The key to applying style . . . is to teach difficult new information through a student's style but also [to] help that student "stretch" by learning through other styles (1990).

With all the learning-style theories that exist, choosing which theory to implement can be a confusing process. Learning styles researcher Pat Guild advocates using a variety of learning-style models. She writes: "The key issues are: people are different, learners will respond differently to a variety of instructional methods, and we need to respect and honor the individual differences among us" (Brandt 1990, 12).

A working knowledge of learning styles allows teachers to adapt instruction to individual differences among students. This might involve using a variety of instructional approaches instead of relying on one that "fits" a particular learning style. Or a teacher might design several assignments that are oriented intentionally to different learning styles—then let students select from among them. This approach both provides students opportunities for choice—thus more actively engaging them in learning—and allows them to select materials, projects, and assignments suited to their own styles of learning. When students are given greater choices in how they learn and opportunities to express their talents, they are more likely to become engaged in learning, thus contributing to an orderly and productive classroom environment.

Students in a single classroom also often vary widely in ability level. Consequently, teachers must provide supplementary instruction for higher achievers to avoid boredom, and for lower achievers to avoid frustration, all the while ensuring the needs of average students are not overlooked. Class activities should be flexible in structure, allowing students to work at their own pace. When working with lower achievers, teachers may need to break instruction into smaller segments, work closely with students to help them develop or improve their study skills, and carefully monitor understanding of the lesson (Arnold and Dodge 1994).

Effective teachers continuously monitor the progress of their students. By monitoring progress on assignments and other work, teachers can note minor problems before they become serious. When problems are noted, teachers can provide additional assistance or re-teach. The teacher also can use information about academic progress to gear the level of instruction to students' levels of knowledge, allowing students to focus on the learning material. Early intervention with instructional problems can prevent students from becoming bored, frustrated, and possibly disruptive.

Providing Instruction in Ways Students Find Interesting

"Busy children are usually good children," notes Greenberg (1992, 13). Instructional strategies can help prevent behavior problems in elementary students if:

- *They're interesting.* Students can become indifferent and rebellious with monotonous routines, old content, and tedious presentations (Palardy 1993).

- *They're matched with your pupils' abilities.* Greenberg (1992) recommends channeling young students' inappropriate classroom behavior into positive classroom contributions by incorporating each child's special abilities—such as a proclivity for comedy, art, talking, and helping—into something from which the whole class can learn.

- *They're matched with your pupils' interests.* Alber and Heward (1996) suggest that teachers turn "inappropriate" interests into positive learning experiences by, for example, occasionally allowing a student to read a comic book rather than literature because she is acquiring the skills needed to be able to read literature.

Think about starting lessons with an activity that includes opportunities for student interaction and so is viewed as "fun." For example, instead of simply stating, "Open your books to Chapter 5," ask students to share information from the previous day's class with a neighbor. Other good ways to start a lesson include giving students an overview or a written list of objectives, or asking them to brainstorm as a class about what they already know about the upcoming topic. A K-W-L (Know-Want to Know-Learned) chart provides a great means for activating students' prior knowledge of a topic, stimulating thinking about new information to be uncovered, and reviewing what was learned during the lesson.

Provide opportunities for interaction. An interactive classroom contains elements such as cooperative groups, role playing, writing ideas on the blackboard, brainstorming, and checking each other's work. Obviously, a classroom routinely providing opportunities for students to work in cooperative groups—as contrasted with one in which the typical approach to instruction is teacher lecture—complicates the teacher's task of monitoring student behavior. However, researchers point out that an interactive classroom can actually minimize disruption and so may actually ease concerns about classroom management (Seeman 1988).

For many students, simply having opportunities to talk about what they are learning and to hear others as well reinforces material presented through teacher lecture or other means. For some, it may help because it more closely matches their preferred learning style. Research on how people learn provides yet another reason why the approach can be effective. Working in groups can fulfill the human need for social interaction. In addition, each student's role in contributing to the group and working toward a common goal creates a powerful purpose for individual learning.

Activities that call for more active involvement on the part of students also can be structured so they foster student cooperation, responsibility, and self-discipline. Another advantage of such an approach is the opportunity it provides for teachers to observe students as they problem solve and apply knowledge. These observations can be important diagnostic tools to help teachers assess who is mastering objectives and who is not.

The way teachers pose questions during lessons also can affect the level of student engagement. It is generally recommended that teachers wait three to five seconds between asking a question and calling on students. Called "wait time," this strategy gives students and teachers time to think, promotes richer responses to questions, and brings in those students who respond more slowly.

Finally, a kindergarten teacher reports she changes activities frequently to provide her students with the opportunity to "get their wiggles out before they start poking their friends when they should be adding 2 plus 2" (Strauss 2002, online).

Moving through the Classroom as You Teach

Teacher mobility is crucial to a productive classroom environment. Research has found that frequent teacher movement throughout the classroom can minimize disruptions (Shore, Gunter, and Jack 1993). Such movement is facilitated by arranging student desks or tables in a manner that allows easy movement throughout the room.

Teacher mobility also can improve the audibility of teacher-student discourse. Students may have difficulty hearing others who are not nearby. For example, when a student who is sitting near the teacher responds to a question, it often appears to be a private conversation between the teacher and student, and other students may not be able to hear. If the teacher moves around as students speak, however, no one group of students is always nearest to the teacher, and all students will routinely need to raise their voices in order to be heard by their classmates. This strategy is particularly effective if the teacher makes a conscious effort to position him- or herself farthest from the student who is talking. Such effort necessitates a change in teaching style, yet may pay off in greater on-task behavior and improved comprehension (Wall 1993).

Managing Cooperative Learning

Though researchers have identified many factors that contribute to well-managed *whole-class* activities, there is limited research on how teachers create a positive, orderly environment when implementing *small-group,* cooperative learning activities. Some educators simply apply whole-class management strategies to small-group settings.

This approach can be effective. One study suggests that many of the techniques important to interactive, small-group instruction are in fact those used in successful traditional classroom environments. These include communicating expectations and goals, devising specific guidelines and limits, giving students opportunities to practice desired behaviors, and planning in advance (Blank and Kershaw 1993).

Yet some management strategies used in conjunction with direct instruction are not compatible with small-group settings or cooperative learning. For instance, the teacher cannot directly supervise the activities of every group all the time, and student talk must be permitted. Also, in order to reach two important goals of cooperative learning—building students' cooperation skills and encouraging students to learn from one another—the teacher must relinquish some control to students, and students must take on more responsibility for managing their behavior and work activities.

An initial step in the shifting of responsibility is introducing exercises that improve cooperation skills, as well as teaching students cooperative norms. (For example, students have the right to ask others in the group for help, and they have the duty to assist others who need help.) Another way to give students responsibility is to develop different roles they can serve within their groups, such as facilitator, materials person, secretary, clean-up person, checker, or timekeeper. Also, research suggests that when noting non-cooperation, teachers refrain from providing a solution, instead giving students a chance to solve the problem. This might be accomplished by telling students the behavior observed, and then asking them to discuss what the problem is and what they want to do about it (Cohen 1991). Again, the emphasis is on student development of self-control.

Though students take on more responsibility, the teacher does not play a smaller role in learning. For example, the teacher must evaluate students in terms of skill levels and assign them to groups accordingly, arrange the physical environment, and prepare instructional materials and equipment. Also, the teacher must help students establish group roles and cooperative norms, stimulate thinking and talking among the students, notice groups that are not cooperating and encourage them to solve the problem, and, in some cases, change groups that are not working out.

Most important, teachers need to be flexible when implementing cooperative learning strategies (Blank and Kershaw 1993). Flexibility is important in terms of scheduling, responding to student interests and suggestions, and thinking about the way students learn best. In addition, teachers may need to overcome fears of appearing too lenient or disorganized if they allow noise or less-structured activities; they must be able to tolerate more noise, movement, peer interaction, and informal structures than in traditional teacher-centered classrooms.

Effective Classroom Management to Support Student Learning

> ## With-it-ness and Overlapping—Important Teacher Skills
>
> With-it-ness is the ability to communicate an awareness of student behavior and to respond quickly to incidents that threaten to become disruptive. In order to have with-it-ness, teachers must regularly monitor the classroom, stationing themselves so all students can be seen, and continuously scan the room. Students soon learn that their teacher is highly attuned to their behavior, which sets high expectations.
>
> Overlapping is the ability to attend to more than one situation at once—a crucial skill, considering the number of events that occur in a classroom on any given day. For example, if a lesson is interrupted by a student coming in late, an effective teacher quickly addresses the situation and then smoothly returns to the lesson at hand. A well-planned lesson makes it simpler for a teacher to overlap, because he/she has a clear idea of where the lesson should be going, even if interrupted. Effective teachers deal with disruptions in the way that is least disruptive to the lesson—optimally with a nonverbal signal or with a brief verbal response (DiGiulio 1995).

Providing Students with Success Experiences

Rewards and good grades may boost student self-confidence, but the best way to ensure student success is by providing students with genuine success experiences. DiGiulio writes:

> Feelings of success come when a student actually does something of value—participating, performing, creating, practicing, designing, producing, carrying out an experiment, finishing an assignment, or any of hundreds of other "doing" activities. In the final analysis, what the student does will have a greater impact on how successful the student is (and feels he or she is) than what the teacher knows, says, or believes (1995, 43).

Other suggestions for providing success experiences include:

- Make use of learning-style ideas, providing students with opportunities to perform in the areas that they have abilities and strengths.

- Gear tasks to the appropriate level of difficulty, optimally just a little beyond students' current achievement levels, so students are challenged. In order to gauge the appropriate level, routinely look over homework and other assignments and assess students' level of understanding.

- Break instruction down into a sequence of steps. When students achieve mastery of the initial steps in the sequence, they are more likely to master advanced steps later. This strategy allows slow learners more time to achieve success, and lets faster learners skip the material they already know (DiGiulio 1995; Walberg and Paik 2004).

Some Special Issues for Today's Classrooms

No one approach or tactic for classroom management is likely to meet all the needs of today's teachers, given the countless number of situations and personalities with which each teacher must contend. While many approaches will produce positive results with some students, no one approach, by itself, is likely to be completely effective. Effective classroom managers have a repertoire of strategies, from which they can select the most suitable for the given situation (Reed 1991).

In light of recent demographic changes in the school-age population, an eclectic approach is now more appropriate than ever before. Students always have varied in terms of ability, personality, and experience, but recent trends have broadened the spectrum that is likely to be found in any one classroom or school. The student population is increasingly multicultural and multilingual. Recent immigrants possess a wide range of life experiences and educational backgrounds, and some speak little or no English. In addition, the current trend toward inclusion has resulted in the placement of increasing numbers of students with emotional or attentional disorders in the regular classroom.

Effective classroom managers recognize that the ethnic backgrounds of students influence their learning patterns, perceptions, communication styles, and behavior. For example, whereas in the United States it is usually expected that students will maintain eye contact when interacting with teachers, in certain cultures prolonged eye contact may signify disrespect or even defiance. Consequently, many African American, Latino, Native American, and Asian American students will not look directly at teachers when they are talking, which teachers may mistakenly interpret as a sign that these students are not paying attention. Yet, they may be listening intently (Gay 2000).

Students from different cultures also may have widely varied perceptions of what constitutes appropriate personal space. And some students are unfamiliar with the custom of raising one's hand to answer a question. When these students call out in class, they may appear to be deliberately misbehaving, when in fact they are simply behaving as they have learned (Johnson and Protheroe 2003).

Weinstein, Curran, and Tomlinson-Clarke provide some specific examples of how cultural differences can lead to teacher misinterpretations of the meaning of student behaviors:

> Maria emigrated from Mexico to the United States when she was five. Now in a third-grade, monolingual English class, she sits quietly at her desk and speaks only when her White, middle-class teacher calls on her. She does, however, raise her hand frequently to ask if she's doing her assignments correctly. Her teacher believes Maria is insecure and overly dependent on her. In class, she often chides her to be more outgoing and independent; she repeated this message on Maria's report card and at parent conferences. Maria's teacher is unaware of the fact that Hispanic parents tend to expect their children to be quiet and obedient in school and to seek advice and approval before acting.

> Houng, a Vietnamese American girl in second grade, repeatedly answers "Yes" when her teacher, Ms. Adams, asks her if she understands. Her written work, however, consistently reveals her confusion. Frustrated and annoyed, Ms. Adams concludes that Houng lacks motivation to learn and chastises her for not seeking help. Ms. Adams has no idea that the literal equivalent of "yes" in Vietnamese is "da," which can also mean "I am politely listening to you" (Grossman in Weinstein, Curran, and Tomlinson-Clarke 2003).

> James is an African American sixth-grader who is loud, active, assertive, and quick to interject comments into a class discussion without raising his hand. His teacher (who is African American and was educated in predominantly White schools) realizes that the school's emphasis on quiet, passivity, and turn taking is strikingly different from the behavioral expectations that exist in James's home; nonetheless, she believes it is important for James to learn "appropriate" classroom behavior. For this reason, she frequently reprimands him, makes him miss recess, and has him stay for detention.

The teachers in all of these situations are interpreting and responding to their students' behavior from the perspective of mainstream sociocultural norms. Although well meaning, these teachers are acting in ways that actually discriminate against students from racial and ethnic minority backgrounds. Such discrimination occurs when teachers do not recognize that behavior is culturally influenced; when they devalue, censure, and punish the behaviors of non-mainstream groups; and when they fail to see that their management practices alienate and marginalize some students, while privileging others (Weinstein, Curran, and Tomlinson-Clarke 2003, online).

While a teacher will obviously need to ensure student behaviors—even those that are culturally related—do not interfere with the flow of learning, a better understanding of cultural differences that may be at the root of some of these behaviors is essential. By better understanding these differences, a teacher may be able to modify some classroom routines to better match a student's expectations and experiences. In addition, this knowledge provides important information about how to more effectively respond to problematic behaviors.

In order for classroom management in culturally diverse classrooms to be effective, teachers need to state rules and expectations as clearly as possible, making sure that students understand the rules, and they need to be aware that what seems to be misbehavior may be the result of a misunderstanding. Increased teacher attention to some typical patterns may assist with correct interpretation of behavior, followed by an appropriate response to that behavior (Johnson and Protheroe 2003).

Behavior and language that are considered inappropriate for the classroom should not be tolerated, however, even if it is the norm in the student's home and community. High expectations for all students are critical to promoting student success.

In brief, given the diversity in today's classrooms, teachers need to recognize individual differences and be willing to "go the extra mile" to help each of their students succeed. Gay suggests teachers first focus on relatively simple changes that could be made to what she terms the "what" and "how" of instructional interactions. These could include:

- Extending wait time and changing turn-taking rules to honor the participation styles of students of different ethnic and cultural backgrounds.

Questions to Identify Cultural Practices that Influence Students' Behaviors

Family Dynamics

- What are the important family rules?

- What are the primary disciplinary methods used at home and the students' reactions to these methods?

- Is the student praised, corrected, or criticized? How often and by whom?

- What are the behavioral expectations for children toward elders and teachers?

- What emotions are expressed openly? What emotions are never expressed?

- What messages are communicated to children nonverbally?

- Are shame and guilt used as disciplinary techniques?

Perceptions about Student Behavior

- What roles do silence, questions, and responses play in the student's culture?

- How do students' quiet and obedient behaviors (e.g., lack of overt responding and calling attention to oneself) affect the teachers' perceptions?

- Do students' inappropriate behaviors result from a lack of language proficiency and/or misunderstanding?

- Does the teaching style (e.g., teacher-directed instruction) differ from the student's accustomed learning style (e.g., peer-mediated instruction)?

Key Elements of Effective Classroom Management

Student Characteristics

- Do students question or obey authority figures?

- Do students assume a competitive or a cooperative posture in their learning and interaction with other students?

- Do students put their needs and desires before those of the group, or vice versa?

- What are the students' beliefs regarding sharing belongings with others? How do these beliefs affect classroom organization and expectations?

- Do boys and girls demonstrate differential behavioral expectations in their interactions with each other or with adults? Do students' perceptions about gender influence grouping patterns in the classroom or their interactions with and respect for authority figures?

- Do students maintain personal space or distance differentially in their interactions with other students of the same gender, opposite gender, or with adults?

Disciplinary Style

- What are acceptable and unacceptable ways to motivate or change students' behaviors, based on their perceptions of positive and negative consequences?

- What are acceptable ways to provide feedback to students about their academic and social behaviors?

- How do students' perceptions about group rights influence their willingness to change behaviors to benefit their peers? (Sileo and Prater 1998, 329).

- Using alternative cues to indicate attending behaviors, such as asking students to summarize points previously made, to restate another's point of view, or to declare their personal preferences on issues under discussion.

- Shortening the length of segments of teacher talk.

- Minimizing teacher talk by using learning strategies that are more student focused and active, such as small-group tasks, simulations, role playing, dramatic readings, and cooperative learning.

- Providing opportunities for students to establish, monitor, manage, and correct their own rules of classroom discourse.

- Honoring students' natural learning styles and ways of learning as much as possible. For example, teachers might encourage students to use cultural styles of storytelling to demonstrate their translation and reading comprehension skills, to present critical incidents in social studies, or to report the results of inquiry exercises or research topics. Teachers might also ask more divergent, higher-order cognitive and affective questions that give all students an opportunity to respond, and then accept students' affective reactions as legitimate contributions to the learning process (2000, 10).

Chapter 4

Promoting Student Self-Management

Ultimately, one goal of classroom management should be to help students internalize responsible behavior so it will occur without reminder and become incorporated into the student's daily life.

An approach that recognizes the importance of student self-management incorporates opportunities that promote self-discipline in the classroom on a daily basis. For example, students could take part in developing rules, work with the teacher to create plans or contracts for assessing and correcting their own behavior, be trained in peer mediation, or have opportunities to select some of their own instructional activities based on their individual learning styles. Students also could be involved in the evaluation of classroom and school processes. This might include participating in class meetings about classroom concerns, providing feedback to teachers, or even evaluating school programs that deal with behavior issues.

Research indicates that training students in self-management has beneficial results such as increasing on-task behavior and reducing attention difficulties. Its effects have been found to hold across different populations of students at different age levels and to generalize across behaviors and tasks (Shapiro and Cole 1994).

Finally, this emphasis on teaching students to be better managers of their own behavior is consistent with a shift in instructional approaches. In recent years, there has been much discussion about the need to change instruction in ways that move the teacher from the role of authority figure to that of guide. This approach encourages students to be more actively involved in the learning process and to assume more responsibility for their own learning. In a similar way, taking an approach to classroom management that promotes student self-management better supports active learning and simultaneously provides students with the opportunity to learn and practice important life skills.

Establishing Guidelines for Acceptable Behavior

Each classroom is a mini-community in which there are typically norms for what is considered acceptable—and unacceptable—behavior. Making these norms explicit through the establishment of "rules" and providing opportunities for student involvement in the development of these rules are important steps in teaching students how to manage their own behavior.

The Role of "Rules"

Classroom rules can serve to promote students' good behavior and so contribute to the development of a classroom community focused on learning. Students need boundaries for their behavior so they learn the importance of managing time, learn right from wrong, and learn how to behave in ways consistent with norms (Fuhr 1993). Students also should be taught that rights in a democracy must be balanced with social responsibilities (Landau and Gathercoal 2000).

The Responsive Classroom approach described by Horsch, Chen, and Nelson emphasizes the importance of rules that are understood by all:

> These classroom management tools are intended to instill "habits of goodness" in children and to promote and sustain community. Developed at the beginning of the school year, rules are positive statements that establish guidelines and expectations for classroom behavior; they are the cornerstones of classroom life and are used to encourage conversation and problem solving related to ethical issues that arise at school. For example, first-grade rules include "Take care of friends and materials" and "Be a good listener and use your words to solve problems" (1999, 224).

Rademacher, Callahan, and Pederson-Seelye offer the following suggestions for the content and use of classroom rules:

- Make them acceptable to both teacher and students. Rules should be reasonable, and they should be changed when conditions change.

- Begin each rule with an action word, and state it in positive terms. For example, "Walk in the halls" is more effective than "Don't run in the halls."

- Focus the rule on observable behaviors (i.e., you can see the behavior associated with the rule). "Raise your hand to be recognized" is observable, while "Think before you speak" is not.

- Have only eight or fewer rules.

- Post rules so that you and your students can easily see them. The visual reminder can help students comply (1998, 286-287).

State rules in positive terms and focus on observable behavior.

While the content of the rules is important, the way in which they are used also has an impact. For example, when a teacher clearly communicates rules and imposes consequences when rules are broken, he/she sends the message that maintaining order is considered important. Other factors that may promote good classroom behavior include phrasing rules in a positive way (telling students what good behavior is) rather than in a restrictive way (telling students what not to do) and giving students a role in writing class rules.

Student Participation in the Development of Rules

Including students in the development of classroom rules serves three important purposes. First, students who feel their opinions have been considered are more likely to behave in accordance with the rules. Second, discussions among students and teachers while developing rules and consequences may help students understand them better. Finally, the process provides students with an opportunity to practice participation in a community—a skill that can be important to them through life. Schimmel (1997) reports on one Washington, D.C., school where all students participate during the first week of school each fall in a structured process of rule-making. The approach uses small group discussion, emphasizes responsibility and cooperation, identifies positive as well as negative consequences of student behavior, and culminates in a formal ceremony in which the teacher and each student signs a "Classroom Constitution."

Castle and Rogers found that students who are given input on designing classroom rules:

> . . . frequently respond to such trust by developing rules that are strikingly similar to, and perhaps even stricter than, those advocated by their teachers. Thus, allowing them to participate in the process

does not so much affect what the rules look like as it does their perceptions of the rules (in Latham 1998, online).

Adolescents often have particular issues with rules: they want and need security and support, but they also want independence from adults (Reed 1991). Involving these students in making classroom rules helps them develop a sense of ownership of the rules—and so be more likely to behave in accordance with them (Palardy 1993).

Additional Ways to Promote the Development of Student Self-Management Skills

Although establishing expectations for student behavior and communicating the expectation students will follow these guides are essential components of a well-managed classroom, some students may need additional support in their efforts to regulate their own behavior. There are ways teachers can help strengthen students' self-management skills that need not take extensive time away from content-area instruction. Wilson provides some examples:

- *Helping particular students gain control over specific behaviors.* This involves either targeting a specific behavior for improvement (such as raising one's hand before speaking), or targeting a behavior for elimination (such as losing one's temper).

- *Giving students a role in solving classroom conflicts.* Students might be selected for training in conflict resolution, or all classmates might work to resolve a problem.

- *Providing students with choices.* Students might be allowed to make choices about what, how, or when they will learn (1996, 32).

Involving Students in "Running" the Classroom

In recent years, many educators and researchers have linked choice with the development of responsibility. For example, Kohn writes:

> . . . if we want children to *take* responsibility for their own behavior, we must first *give* them responsibility, and plenty of it. The way a child learns how to make decisions is by making decisions, not by following directions (1993, 11).

Lessons from Research

Students' interpersonal skills can be built through practice—and schools can help with this.

Research findings: Children learn interpersonal skills in various ways. They observe parents, teachers, and peers handle situations and learn from what they see. Adults also instruct children in how to behave. One thing is clear from research on teaching children to resist peers' encouragement to use tobacco, alcohol, and drugs, however: adult instruction is not enough. Practicing the skills is crucial, too. Children must also generalize what they have learned to real-life situations. Teaching children how to handle problem situations will be most effective if it involves: (a) instruction and opportunities to observe others behave effectively, (b) practice and feedback on the skills they are learning, (c) instruction in many different examples of the skills, and (d) positive consequences from adults or peers when children use their skills in their daily lives. In addition, children must learn skills that fit their culture and will help them be more effective in the situations they encounter.

In Schools

- Teachers should act in ways that show children how to handle problems well. Children imitate the behavior of those who are important to them. Teach young children interpersonal skills for handling conflict nonviolently and cooperating with others. Children can also benefit from learning cognitive skills for recognizing problem situations, stopping to think rather than responding impulsively, generating ways of solving problems, and evaluating the consequences of different solutions.

- Teach young adolescents specific ways for handling situations in which peers invite or pressure them to use drugs, tobacco, or alcohol or to become involved in delinquency activities or risky sexual behavior.

- Incorporate teaching interpersonal skills into classroom teaching. Make sure children have many opportunities to practice the skills they are learning and to receive feedback on how they are doing.

- Train children to use skills that are likely to be effective in real-life situations. Whenever possible, make sure they receive positive consequences for using their skills. Children are likely to abandon what they have learned if they try a new behavior and it fails to work for them.

- Children who have problems getting along with others are likely to have more difficulties than others with learning and mastering important interpersonal skills. They may need more practice and feedback than others and more systematic attempts to help them apply what they have learned (Foster et al. 2002).

Choices might be provided simply by giving students opportunities throughout the day or class period to make decisions about how they will learn. For example, students might be offered the chance to choose the books they will read, where they will sit while they work, whether to discuss a story in small groups or as a whole class, or whether to study math before or after recess.

Another way of teaching students responsibility is to involve them in resolving classroom problems. This can be done in the form of a classroom discussion, in which problems of concern to all are addressed. For example, if student noise during small-group work is disturbing classmates who are silently reading, the class can discuss approaches that better allow for both types of activities.

Classroom meetings give teachers and students an opportunity to share thoughts, identify problems, consider possible solutions, develop a plan of action, and then evaluate the success of the solution. In order for a classroom meeting to be successful, all students must feel as though they are participants—even if not everyone has the opportunity to talk. There should be a few clear guidelines—such as avoiding name calling or calling ideas "stupid"—that are applied consistently. In addition, the teacher initially may need to highlight times when the discussion wanders so students learn to stay focused on addressing the problem.

There are a variety of frameworks for addressing classroom problems and many possible roles for teachers and students. Kohn (1993) provides some approaches:

- teacher and students take turns deciding on solutions to problems;
- teacher offers suggestions and guidance, but leaves the final choice to students;
- teacher provides students with a few specific possibilities from which they can choose; and
- teacher specifies the goal, but allows students to choose how they will reach the goal.

Responsibility Training, a strategy developed by Jones (1987), recognizes the importance of choice to the development of self-discipline. Jones contends that—for students to learn to be responsible members of the classroom community—they must view themselves as exercising control over a classroom resource such as time. In addition, they should have to live with the consequences of their actions in regard to the resource.

He suggests introducing the concept of "preferred activity time" (PAT). Preferred activity time should *not* be a normal class activity such as recess or time to finish assignments. Nor should it be free time for students to relax and do their own activities. Rather, it should be an entirely new addition to the classroom, with its main purpose being the enjoyment of learning. For example, PAT might be time to engage in a fun and educational computer program, or time to play a game-show-style activity that relates to the topics being studied.

To begin the process, the teacher allocates a specified amount of preferred activity time. The class can earn bonus amounts of PAT for good behavior or getting tasks done quickly, but it can also lose PAT if the class doesn't remain on task due to misbehavior or disruption. Rather than nagging students when they are misbehaving, the teacher simply pauses for a moment and demonstrates he/she is keeping track of how much time is lost. The amount of time consumed by the misbehavior is then subtracted from the preferred activity time. By explicitly connecting the loss of PAT to time wasted due to misbehavior or disruption, the teacher demonstrates the importance of students' taking responsibility for their actions if they want the opportunity to engage in a "fun" activity.

Teaching Conflict Resolution Skills

Instruction also can be used to teach children basic conflict resolution strategies—another important element in the development of self-management. Shifting the responsibility for resolving some conflicts to students frees time for teachers to focus on instruction rather than discipline (Bodine and Crawford 1998). In addition, conflict resolution training improves important life skills such as listening, critical thinking, and problem solving.

Many conflict resolution programs deliver training and practice in three problem-solving strategies: negotiation, mediation, and consensus decision making. In negotiation, the parties meet face-to-face and work together, without assistance, to resolve their dispute. Mediation differs from negotiation in that the parties are joined by a mediator, a neutral third party who resolves the dispute. Consensus decision making is a group problem-solving process in which all disputants meet to collaboratively develop a plan of action to resolve the dispute; it may or may not be facilitated by a mediator (Bodine and Crawford 1998).

Effective Classroom Management to Support Student Learning

"Though the responsibility of maintaining equilibrium in the classroom rests with the teacher, it's often the collective wisdom of a bunch of kids with good problem solving skills that can restore a classroom's harmony" (Vuko 2003, C9).

While some schools introduce training in conflict resolution either schoolwide or for particular grades, teachers also can embed instruction about the principles in students' normal academic work. For example, some teachers use controversy as an instructional tool that can simultaneously teach content and skills needed for conflict resolution. To implement this approach, the teacher selects an issue for discussion, places students in cooperative learning groups, and assigns students divergent positions to advocate through organizing information and deriving conclusions. Students then present their positions, challenge the positions of other groups, and search for additional information to view the issue from both perspectives simultaneously.

When used in a noncompetitive context, the approach has been found to provide academic benefits while enhancing students' ability to see more than one side of an issue (Johnson and Johnson 1995). Once students have experience with resolving academic conflicts successfully, they may be better able to resolve everyday classroom conflicts.

Burnett describes four steps to conflict resolution that can be taught even to young children:

1. *Identify the problem without blame.* Focus on the conflict without placing blame on one person for the situation. For example, "William says that you called him a put-down name, Juanita. Is it ever okay to call someone a bad name?"

2. *Brainstorm alternatives together.* You might ask, "William, what do you think is a good amount of time to be on a swing? Juanita, what do you think should happen if one student has been on the swing a long time and another student has been waiting for a turn?"

3. *Agree on a solution.* Ask students to state which possible solution they think would most likely work for all concerned. For example,

"William, what would be a fair way to share the swings? Juanita, do you agree that five minutes is a long-enough time?"

4. *Evaluate the result.* Schedule a follow-up meeting for the next day, when everyone reviews whether the suggested behaviors were followed (2000, 20-22).

Peer mediation is another approach to moving more responsibility for behavior management to students. Peer mediation programs teach students practical ways to deal with day-to-day conflicts such as name-calling and gossip. Using peer mediation, students can settle disputes among themselves without interrupting the entire class. A basic tenet of these programs is that conflict can be constructive, if the issues are dealt with through reasoned discussion. Many school mediation programs report positive results, such as improved problem-solving skills, fewer student-to-student conflicts, and fewer discipline referrals to the central office (Eisler, Lane, and Mei 1995; Ikram and Bratlien 1994; Johnson and Johnson 1995; Johnson et al.1992; Lane and McWhirter 1992).

Mediators are trained in active listening, cooperation, acceptance of differences, creative problem-solving, and remaining impartial and nonjudgmental in the face of conflict. The task of the mediator is to determine what happened, how the parties involved feel about it, and what they would like to see happen in the future (Hamby 1995). The mediator should make sure each side understands the point of view of the other side, ask the students involved to identify how the problem might be resolved, help the students come to a mutual agreement about what they are willing to do, and then have them sign a statement of the agreement.

Working with Individual Students

When the strategies described above are implemented classwide, they provide both instruction and opportunities to practice acceptable behavior for most students. However, students who are more likely to be off task, disruptive, or otherwise engage in undesirable behavior may need special attention. Two possible interventions are self-monitoring and self-instruction training. More often used with students who are learning disabled or have behavioral disorders, they also have been shown to be effective in regular education settings (Prater 1994).

Steps for training students in self-monitoring procedures include:

- Defining the behaviors to be monitored. Include the student's input in defining goals, setting criteria, and setting contingencies. Develop brief written descriptions or visual representations for student use as reminders or references.

- Designing a system that accurately measures behavior and is easy for students to use, such as a chart that can be seen by all students.

- Describing and modeling self-management procedures. The student should also have opportunities to describe the undesired behavior.

- Assessing the accuracy of the student's observations about the occurrence or nonoccurrence of behavior during a "training period." This can be done by matching the student's observations against the teacher's observations and providing positive reinforcement for accurate recording. A high student-teacher level of agreement (about 80 percent) should be obtained before the student is considered trained.

- Planning for generalization of behavior by providing opportunities for self-recording in other classes, at other times of day.

- Gradually withdrawing the prompt and the self-recording procedure as the student's behavior approaches the goal, while ensuring the improved behavior is maintained (Carter 1993; Prater 1994).

According to Johnson and Johnson (1999), this procedure has been found to help students become more independent and self-directed while reducing the amount of time the teacher spends responding to misbehavior.

Self-instruction training involves teaching a student verbalizations that help guide him or her through tasks or behaviors. For example, students prone to fighting can be taught verbalizations to deal with peers who are taunting them. These students might be instructed to (1) stop, (2) count to 10 slowly, and (3) think before reacting (Prater 1994). As an important related benefit, students can be taught to generalize and apply the new skills to instructional challenges. For example, some low-achieving students typically may respond too quickly to a question or assignment and should be encouraged to "think before reacting."

Self-instruction training often is most effective when coupled with self-monitoring. For example, a student who has difficulty controlling her temper could record the occurrence of losing her temper and also take explicit notice of how well different strategies help to control feelings of anger or frustration.

For both approaches, the behaviors should be well defined, the student should be trained in the use of the procedure with modeling and role playing, and the teacher should provide opportunities for the student to generalize his/her behavior to other situations.

Chapter 5

Dealing with Problem Behaviors

Dealing effectively with challenging behaviors can have a significant impact on the teaching-learning environment—as well as on the behavior of other students. More than three of every four teachers questioned in a Public Agenda survey are of the opinion, "if it weren't for discipline problems, I could be teaching a lot more effectively," with 40 percent saying they strongly agree with the statement (2004, 9).

Today's classrooms and schools seem significantly more likely to be affected by students who bring frustration, anger, conflict, and behavioral or attention problems with them—and who do not have skills to deal effectively with these emotions. Some of these students just can't seem to pay attention or sit still, while others may be actual discipline problems. The result is the same—they make it more difficult to focus on teaching and learning for themselves and for other students. So what is a teacher to do?

Although the suggestions already discussed help develop a framework for a smoothly run classroom—one in which there are seldom disruptions caused by student misbehavior—it would be naïve to assume these commonsense approaches would eliminate all problems. In almost every classroom—every year—there is at least one student whose behavior challenges even the most talented and patient teacher. These challenges must be dealt with if that student, as well as other students in the class, are to have days focused on learning.

As a starting point, it is important teachers try to understand factors that may underlie challenging student behaviors. Feeling angry and out of control is not a pleasant experience for a student—nor are many of the life experiences that may have developed these response tendencies. Other students may have attention problems and disrupt the flow of learning by off-task behaviors. Any of these students—while a challenge to their teachers—may be even more of a problem for themselves than for others in part because they typically receive little positive feedback.

Expectations, Caring, and Consistency

None of the suggestions provided in this *What We Know About* assumes that dealing with disruptive behavior is easy. It requires skill, patience, and energy. However, there are three additional words that should be highlighted in this discussion. The first is expectations. Teachers who express high expectations for student behavior and who make these expectations clear are providing an important framework for all students and especially for students who may have had little experience with the concept of limits in their home lives.

The second word is caring. Some students exhibiting disruptive behaviors may have too few positive relationships with adults. While it sometimes may be difficult, teachers need to communicate the message that the misbehavior—not the student—is the problem. Hall and Hall emphasize the importance of relationship building to effective classroom management in general and especially to working with students who exhibit challenging behaviors:

> Building relationships with students who have challenging behaviors is consistent with an emerging paradigm in education. In the old paradigm, educators developed behavior programs designed to squelch students' inappropriate behaviors, a process that focused on what the student was doing wrong. Educators assumed that when they had brought the inappropriate behaviors under control, the student would automatically demonstrate socially appropriate behaviors…. In contrast, a relationship-building approach helps the student develop positive, socially appropriate behaviors by focusing on what the student is doing right (2003, 63).

Finally, consistency is key. In addition to clearly stating expectations for behavior as well as consequences for misbehavior, teachers who consistently apply rules demonstrate the standards apply to all students. These teachers also strengthen students' understanding of their own actions as the triggers for the consequences.

By demonstrating acceptance for the student while using effective techniques for addressing the challenging behavior, a teacher can provide support for the student—and get classroom learning back on track. Porch and Protheroe (2002) suggest that something as simple as meeting and warmly greeting each student at the door every day can make a difference for students who misbehave primarily to get attention.

Taking a Proactive Approach

Many of the good teaching/good classroom management strategies presented also represent proactive efforts to decrease discipline problems. In the view of Porch and Protheroe:

> In part, proactive approaches are successful because they make expectations clear and so decrease the likelihood that students will "misbehave" simply because they misunderstand the boundaries between acceptable and unacceptable behavior. In addition, because the general level of behavior . . . is likely to be more positive, it is easier to focus on the needs of students with moderate to severe behavior problems (2002, 6).

As was suggested in a previous chapter, the most effective guard against misbehavior is good instruction. For example, Churchward suggests that an important tool for classroom teachers—especially in regard to challenging students—is the effective use of focusing techniques when beginning lessons:

> Be sure you have the attention of everyone in your classroom before you start your lesson. Don't attempt to teach over the chatter of students who are not paying attention. Inexperienced teachers sometimes think that, by beginning their lesson, the class will settle down. The students will see that things are underway now and it is time to go to work. Sometimes this works, but [some students] are also going to think that you are willing to compete with them. You don't mind talking while they talk. You are willing to speak louder so that they can finish their conversation even after you have started the lesson. They get the idea that you accept their inattention and that it is permissible to talk while you are presenting a lesson.
>
> The focusing technique means that you will demand their attention before you begin. That you will wait and not start until everyone has settled down (n.d., online).

There also are instructional approaches that can provide students with opportunities to learn about and practice acceptable behavior patterns. For example, through cooperative learning groups, students learn how to work with, share resources with, and help others. In addition, carefully constructed cooperative learning experiences promote greater student efforts to achieve more positive relationships among students, and greater self-esteem and social competence

Effective Classroom Management to Support Student Learning

(Johnson and Johnson 1995). Finally, Wise (2003) suggests organizing opportunities for disruptive students to excel through service activities in the classroom or elsewhere in the school. These opportunities may help them channel their energies more productively and also build a more positive sense of self.

Taking a "Scientific" Approach

Lindberg, Kelley, and Swick suggest teachers should "be scientific" in planning strategies to minimize the disruptive behavior of challenging students. For example, teachers should ask themselves:

- Where can I seat the student to be surrounded by positive role models?

- How can I coordinate reward and consequence systems with the other teachers and the student(s) involved?

- Can I enlist the help of family members in positive ways to improve behavior? (2005, 36).

They go on to provide other suggestions for teachers:

Be careful not to set up the challenging student—in other words, do your best to keep from placing that person in a situation where he or she will surely find trouble. For example, if a student can't resist talking to everybody about everything, don't seat him or her near the pencil sharpener where others will surely be stopping by during the class.

Watch like a hawk for appropriate behavior on the part of the challenging student—catch the student being good. Sincerely compliment whenever you can (remember, private compliments are often more effective with high school students) (2005, 36).

Dealing with Challenging Behaviors

Teachers need to take direct steps to deal with misbehavior or with students who are more likely to misbehave than most. Some of these students also may need more intensive help to modify problem behaviors. Black provides a description that is probably familiar to most teachers:

> Aggressive kids . . . may be highly skilled in fighting, bullying, intimidating, harassing, and manipulating others. But they are deficient in negotiating differences, dealing appropriately with accusations or blame, and responding even-handedly to failure, teasing, rejection, and anger (2003, 45).

Wise talks about the difficulty of working with students who misbehave because their reactions are atypical—for example, they seem to *want* calls made to parents. These students':

> need for attention is met by creating chaos; the need for competence is met by being the biggest bully in the class; the need for recognition is met by being a gang member and having other gang members look up to you (2003, 2).

Some students have never learned appropriate ways to deal with frustration, conflict, or anger. Erk (1999) describes some of the social skills these students may be lacking:

- basic interaction skills, such as making eye contact, using the correct voice level or tone, and taking turns in conversation;
- "getting-along" skills, such as using polite words, helping others, and not violating others' social space or privacy;
- "making friends" skills, such as smiling appropriately, complimenting others, and expressing interest in others' welfare; and
- social coping skills, such as reacting appropriately when someone says "no," coping with frustration or anger, responding to teasing, and understanding that not all social situations go right.

In Erk's view, modeling such behaviors and providing all students with opportunities to practice them as part of the normal classroom routine can be helpful. In addition, there are other approaches that can be implemented in whole-class settings—perhaps with assistance from a school counselor or during health instruction:

- Help children learn to read personal signals that they are feeling angry or are on the edge of losing control. Physiological responses include a faster heartbeat, heavy breathing, feeling flushed or hot, sweatiness, grinding teeth, or tense muscles.... It also may be helpful for students to develop their own "anger meters," which allow them to identify what they feel as they move toward an out-of-control state.

- Train students how to identify an appropriate anger outlet and provide some options—such as a time-out/relaxation chair toward the back of the classroom—for students who periodically need them.

- Teach relaxation techniques such as pausing before acting, taking deep breaths, or doing calm-down counting.

- Help students identify at least one person inside or outside school they feel comfortable talking with when they feel anxious or angry.

- Help students explore possibilities of problematic situations, then work together to generate possible solutions to solve the problems.

- Use books, stories, and videos about anger to help students understand and effectively manage their own frustration, anger, and conflicts. Use writing or art assignments to provide students with opportunities to explore.

- Encourage parental support by providing workshops for parents on dealing with anger and aggression. Enlist the support of other school staff to educate parents about community services that can provide more intensive education and services (Nichtor 2002).

Looking for "Triggers" to Misbehavior

A key to decreasing misbehavior by a specific student is identifying possible triggers for the misbehavior—and then removing or decreasing the frequency with which the triggers occur because:

> Teachers are responsible for, and can alter, the conditions in their classrooms.... When students display undesirable behaviors in the classroom, it is the teacher's responsibility to attempt to find the classroom stimuli that may contribute to the undesirable behavior. Such classroom stimuli may be the type and difficulty level of academic material, the physical classroom arrangement, or the teacher's own behavior (Gunter et al. 1994, 38).

This can be done informally by asking: "what was happening just before the student acted out?" An alternative is to use a more formal approach—such as a functional behavioral assessment matrix (see figure 1)—to collect information on triggers to misbehavior as well as the types of misbehavior that are observed.

The matrix—or a similar recording device—provides the classroom teacher with a quick approach to keeping track of behaviors exhibited by a student. Often, the most productive way to begin working with a student exhibiting problematic behaviors is to step back and look at the context in which the behaviors occur. A brief checklist could be used to help keep track of what happens and—just as important—when it happens. For example, a student who has a low tolerance for repetitive tasks may act out more often when asked to do worksheets of mathematics problems.

> **Often, the most productive way to begin working with a student exhibiting problematic behaviors is to step back and look at the context in which the behaviors occur.**

Although a functional behavior assessment typically is used with students who have been found eligible for special education services and who have been

Figure 1—Functional Behavior Assessment Matrix

Observed Behaviors	Transition	Large group lecture	Small group	Independent work	Paper-pencil	Worksheet-workbook	Read aloud	Read silently	Instructional game	Media	Other
Off-task											
Out-of-seat											
Talk-out											
Non-compliant											
Other											

Code: ☐ = no behavior   ◩ = low rates of behavior   ■ = persistent behavior

Source: Center for Effective Collaboration and Practice 2000, online.

exhibiting inappropriate behavior, it is a good tool to use with any student with behavior problems because it:

> . . . looks beyond the behavior itself. The focus, when conducting a functional behavioral assessment, is on identifying significant, pupil-specific social, affective, cognitive, and/or environmental factors associated with the occurrence (and non-occurrence) of specific behaviors. This broader perspective offers a better understanding of the function or purpose behind student behavior. Behavioral intervention plans based on an understanding of "why" a student misbehaves are extremely useful in addressing a wide range of problem behaviors (Center for Effective Collaboration and Practice 2000, online).

For example, extended periods of seatwork may be identified as a trigger for a student exhibiting hyperactivity or impulsive behavior. By building periodic opportunities for movement or interaction into instruction, a teacher might decrease the likelihood of disruptive behavior by the student. For example, a teacher could provide support by:

- Structuring some classroom discussions in ways that allow for frequent responses from all students—for example, having the whole class give choral responses or having students hold up "true" or "false" cards to indicate their responses to factual questions.

- Making sure the student with hyperactivity has opportunities for physical activities. Build physical movement into the student's routine. Involve him or her in active tasks such as passing out paper, erasing the board, and taking messages to the office. Do not take away daily recess as a consequence for misbehavior or incomplete work (Booth n.d.; Sumpter and Kidd 1998).

In Brock's view (2000), the analysis of "antecedents" may identify factors in the school environment that "set up the child for success or failure." In addition, carefully studying what happens *after* the undesirable behavior (for example, the student typically is able to avoid an unpleasant task by misbehaving) also may help the teacher to break the link and so discourage the misbehavior.

Although specifically talking about students with attention deficit disorders, Brock provides another suggestion for dealing with behavior problems:

Dealing with Problem Behaviors

When Behavior Problems Seem to Take Over the Class: Tips for Teachers

Before effective changes can occur, you need to get to the root of the problem. To do so, you will need to evaluate yourself and your classroom routines as well as the students. To help you zero in on the problem, answer the five W's below:

- Who is a major behavior problem in the class?
- When does chaos tend to break out? (time of day, subject, teaching strategy, etc.)
- What do I do when behavior starts to fall apart? (yell, send out students, etc.)
- Where are the behavior problems most often occurring? (walking to the cafeteria, in the back corner of the room, etc.)
- Why are these behaviors happening?

Once you have zeroed in on problem areas, develop a systematic plan for change. You will need to put serious thought into your plans as well as be diligent in your implementation and consistent in your follow-through. Finally, be patient. Your students' behavior will improve, but it will take time and a considerable amount of effort on your part. Here are some ideas:

- Start the class over by reintroducing the rules and expectations. Pay particular attention to those areas that have been problematic in the past. For instance, if you find that behavior tends to fall apart during transition between activities, restate the rules and expectations before a transition.

Just like the old song says, you need to "accentuate the positive, eliminate the negative." Let's face it, with all the chaos going on in the classroom, there has probably been very little time to notice anything positive. Force yourself to pay attention to what is going *right*—a student who always sits quietly while others are out of control, or even the few minutes at the beginning of the class when the students are all actually in their seats and quiet. When you notice something good, don't keep it to yourself. Let your students know what you saw and like so they can begin to feel better about the class as well. Once you change your perspective, you will be pleasantly surprised to see that your students will also become less negative (Lindberg, Kelley, and Swick 2005, 97).

Management should first target the specific problem behavior. Next, an alternative behavior, incompatible with the problem behavior, should be selected. It is important to keep both behaviors in mind. Not only do we want to make it clear to students what behavior is unacceptable (what we don't want them to do), we also want to make it clear what behavior is acceptable (what we want them to do).

These behaviors should be carefully defined so that the teacher will be able to accurately monitor them…. [Both] antecedents and consequences of both the problem and replacement behaviors need to be studied (2000).

Finally, teachers should realize that the interventions they are using may sometimes "serve to reinforce rather than deter the problem behavior" (Bae 2002, 213). Abrams and Segal suggest teachers ask themselves:

if students modeling aggressive behavior are reinforced, either positively (through attention from staff or peers, or getting their way), or negatively (by escaping or avoiding aversive stimuli, such as removal from a boring or frustrating class) (1998, 11).

If teachers find that they overreact to specific students—for example, sometimes turning little disagreements into a battle of wills—Kottler (2002) suggests they do some self-examination to try to diagnose why these students push their buttons.

Taking a Strategic Approach to Misbehavior

Misbehavior still will occur in spite of preventive classroom management strategies. At that point, it is important to work toward getting—and keeping—all students back on track. Effective teachers recognize that there are gradations of misbehavior and respond strategically. In addition to "saving" strong responses for serious instances of misbehavior, this approach typically has the added advantage of being less disruptive to the instructional flow of the classroom.

An important first step—although sometimes difficult if a particular student oftens exhibits misbehavior—is to stay in control of your own responses. If the student asks, "What did I do?" simply and calmly note the infraction but move on with a minimum of fuss. Do not give the student undue attention and power for misbehavior. Wait until after class to discuss the incident and remind the student of the consequences of breaking the rule. This approach spares limited class time, avoids rewarding misbehavior with more attention, and yet follows up with consequences (Teaching Today n.d.). In general, Bicard suggests using the "least intrusive procedures first" (2000, 39) when dealing with discipline problems.

It also helps to maintain a sense of how the student might view a teacher's specific reaction to the misbehavior. For example, even if the specific teacher response is appropriate, will the student view it as an overreaction? Or will he view it as embarrassing or even humiliating? For these reasons, the "how" of the teacher response is often as important as the "what."

The following discussion of basic strategies for responding to misbehavior presents milder forms of intervention first.

Ignoring Behavior. Not every misbehavior is disruptive enough to merit a response (short and isolated periods of daydreaming, for example). In these cases, it may in fact be more disruptive for the teacher to interrupt the lesson and discipline the student. In addition, ignoring behavior is sometimes a *strategic* intervention, because it may decrease occurrences of unwanted behavior by students who primarily want attention (Buck 1992; Shockley and Sevier 1991) or quickly stop the misbehavior once it begins because the student sees that the teacher will not be "baited" (Hewitt 1999).

Use Nonverbal Cues. Nonverbal responses are often a productive response to misbehavior. In addition to allowing the lesson to flow smoothly, they may be more likely to preserve the student's dignity because they are less "public" recognitions of the misbehavior. Petrie et al. (1998) suggest teachers practice the following nonverbal techniques:

- use space intentionally; for example, stand near the student or move toward the student or around the room;
- use facial and body cues such as eye contact; smiling, frowning, or a stern look; or arms crossed;
- vary voice tone, pitch, or rhythm; and
- vary the degree of perceived or psychological closeness—for example, by touching the student's book.

Some Tips for Reacting to Misbehavior

- Be selective in punishing students for misbehavior. Sometimes a student is bored or simply wants attention. Try to involve the student in another activity or ask the student to explain an idea or concept.

- Decide what is really "bad" behavior. Don't punish students for everything!

- Keep a sense of humor. Sometimes students are trying to be funny, not bad.

- React calmly to disruptive behavior. Students like to "push buttons."

- Make the consequences for misbehavior consistent.

- Communicate the message that students are responsible for their behavior (Tanner et al. 1999, 37).

Verbal Response. A public warning should be a step taken only if there is no other alternative—or if it is clear most of the rest of the class needs the message as well. If this is the case, make sure the delivery of the warning is "clear and businesslike" (DiGiulio 1995, 61). Reprimands are more effective when they are short and to the point, since Abramowitz, O'Leary, and Futtersak (1988) found long reprimands are more likely than short ones to encourage talking back. Finally, when reprimanding, identify an alternative, preferred behavior when possible, such as, "Terrence, look at the blackboard and not outside."

Dealing with More Serious Behavior Problems

Some students "drive you crazy in many ways," says Kottler. "They challenge your authority. They question your competence, and have you doing the same. They may be either so disruptive that it's hard to get much done or so withdrawn they seem impervious to anything you could do" (2002, 1). In his view, some students may be misbehaving in part because they "desperately need to be held within reasonable boundaries" (2002, 10). In dealing with these students, Kottler suggests that teachers:

Dealing with Problem Behaviors

Using Humor

Humor is a potentially effective strategy for dealing with student misbehavior. It can be used strategically to defuse a tense situation, spare hurt feelings, allow teachers or students to "save face" during a spiraling conflict, or redirect attention to more constructive feelings and behaviors (Carlson and Peterson 1995). In addition, humor is perceived by students as an important quality of a good teacher. One example of teacher use of humor after her students had witnessed a schoolyard fight is described below:

> After the bloodied boys passed my open classroom door on their way to being escorted to the principal's office, I shook my head and said to my students, "If you're going to box, at least get paid for it!" Julie added, "Yeah, and make sure you got Blue Cross, man!" The students and I laughed, and it served as a springboard for a class discussion. Instead of moralizing about the evils of fighting, and instead of condoning fighting as a way of resolving differences, I made my point using irony, which resulted in discussion and a teachable moment for my class (DiGiulio 1995, 59).

Several cautions about using humor interventions should be made, however. First, while humor can be effective, sarcasm is not. Such a response can create power struggles that escalate the problem. Secondly, some students may view certain attempts at humor as embarrassing. Knowing the student is as important with humor interventions as with other types of interventions.

- Work on your relationship first. If you have some semblance of dialogue and respect between you, it is far more likely that you can influence things.
- Whenever possible, handle the problem yourself rather than calling others, which risks compromising your authority.
- If possible, handle censures privately so that there is no public loss of face.

Tileston suggests teachers develop plans for how they will handle misbehavior because "when you have a plan, it is more likely that you will not explode or say something that will be difficult to follow up" (2004, 34). A key element in planning ahead is separating the person from the problem. Ask yourself: how will I deal with problem X? If possible, take time to practice reactions with colleagues so that a well-thought-out response becomes almost automatic.

Marzano (2003) also suggests teachers become better informed about both problematic behavior patterns and some teacher reactions to such patterns. For example, an effective—and proactive—intervention for a student who exhibits hostile behaviors may be to provide opportunities for the student to assume classroom responsibilities that allow him to be recognized for that instead of the hostility.

Marzano and Marzano (2003) provide some general guidelines for teachers responding to a student's disruptive behavior. They explain that teachers should use techniques that project assertiveness, not aggressiveness; for example, they suggest teachers should:

- Use assertive body language by maintaining an erect posture, facing the offending student but keeping enough distance so as not to appear threatening and matching the facial expression with the content of the message being presented to students.

- Use an appropriate tone of voice, speaking clearly and deliberately in a pitch that is slightly but not greatly elevated from normal classroom speech . . .

- Persist until students respond with the appropriate behavior . . . do not be diverted by a student denying, arguing, or blaming, but listen to legitimate explanations (2003, online).

Walker, Colvin, and Ramsey (1995) provide a graphic—the acting-out behavior cycle (see page 62)—that can be used to understand a sequence sometimes seen in more severe instances of student misbehavior. By responding appropriately, a teacher can lower the "peak" of the cycle. For example, during the "acceleration phase," teachers should avoid using escalating prompts, project calm, and provide a "face-saving" way out for the misbehaving student.

Wright also recognizes the importance of teacher behaviors to de-escalate problem behavior and emphasizes the need for teachers to "dodge the power trap." In his view, a power struggle can too quickly escalate into a confrontation:

Handling Disruptive Behavior Effectively

Shaughnessy, Coughlin, and Smith asked high school administrators to identify the characteristics of teachers who were effective in dealing with disruptive behavior. These teachers typically:

- handle problems on their own with confidence, professionalism, and a positive attitude;
- communicate clearly and use active listening skills;
- demonstrate concern for student success;
- are respected and trusted by students for their fairness;
- set firm, fair, and consistent limits;
- try to discover the causes of problems;
- keep students on task and actively involved;
- respond immediately to potentially disruptive situations;
- avoid power struggles;
- develop and use a pre-arranged plan of action;
- model correct behavior;
- teach responsibility and let students participate in making decisions about rules and consequences;
- are selective about the battles they take on;
- allow students to save face;
- use effective nonverbal communication;
- circulate and use proximity control;
- provide appropriate alternate behaviors;
- get students back on task after a disruption;
- use the disruptive behavior as a teaching tool; and
- change teacher behavior if necessary (excerpted from 1997, 43-44).

Figure 2—Acting-Out Behavior Cycle

1. Calm
2. Trigger
3. Agitation
4. Acceleration
5. Peak
6. De-escalation
7. Recovery

(Intensity vs. Time)

Source: Walker, Colvin, and Ramsey 1995.

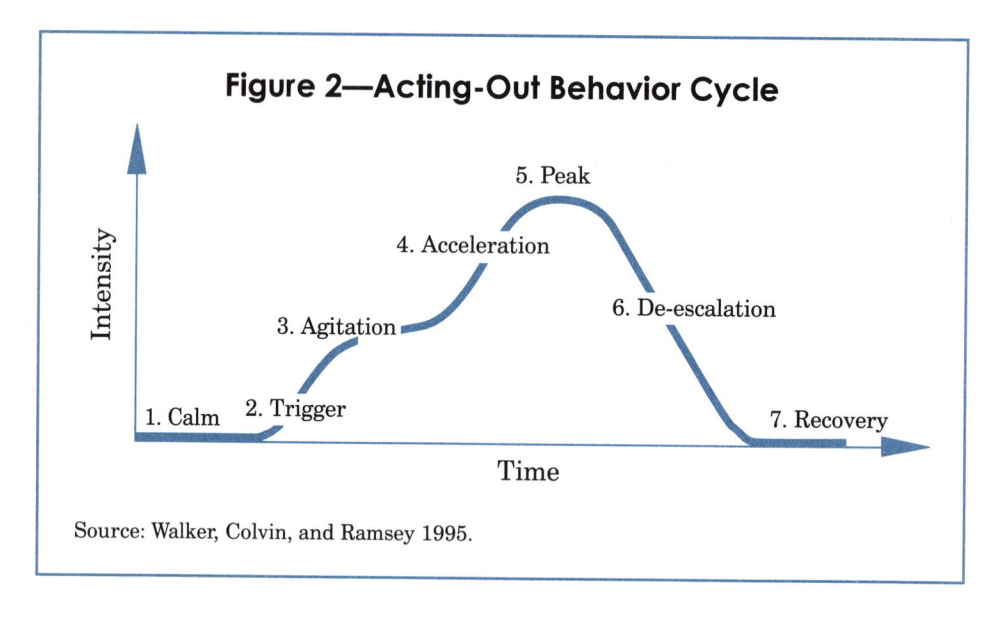

The teacher's most important objective when faced with a defiant or non-compliant student is to remain outwardly calm. Educators who react to defiant behavior by becoming visibly angry, raising their voices, or attempting to intimidate the student may actually succeed only in making the student's oppositional behavior worse!.... Remember: any conflict requires at least two people. A power struggle can be avoided if the instructor does not choose to take part in that struggle (n.d., online).

Wright suggests three categories of tactics that "may calm an oppositional student [although] their main purpose is to help the teacher to keep his or her cool" (n.d., online):

- *Disengaging tactics* are those that allow the teacher to keep his or her cool in order to manage the conflict situation in a professional manner. However, these tactics are not an excuse for educators to look the other way and refuse to get involved when students are misbehaving. Examples include: using stress reduction techniques such as taking a deep breath and releasing it slowly; keeping responses brief and not nagging or using reprimands that may elicit negative student responses; avoiding reaction to mildly annoying comments and responding to comments serious enough to require a response by briefly stating in a neutral manner why the comment was inappropriate and then moving on.

- *Interrupting tactics* are intended to interrupt the escalation of student anger. Interrupting tactics should be positive and respectful in nature. A teacher who tries to shout down or talk over a defiant student is more likely to inflame the confrontation than to calm it. Examples include: diverting the student's attention from the conflict to a more positive topic or behavior such as reading a high-interest book; providing the student with a cool-down break followed by a teacher-student conversation; or paraphrasing essential points of the student's concerns to communicate understanding.

- *De-escalating tactics* are intended to reduce the sense of defensiveness that the student may be experiencing and lower the emotional tension between teacher and student. Teachers who use these calming tactics, however, should not allow students to escape appropriate disciplinary consequences for their behavior. An instructor might decide, for example, to postpone disciplining an aggressive or confrontational student until he or she manages to lower that student's level of anger. After the behavioral outburst is over, though, that teacher should arrange a conference with the student to debrief about the incident and impose any disciplinary steps that seem warranted. Examples include: replacing negative words in teacher requests with positive words; using non-verbal strategies such as sitting next to the student instead of standing over him; providing the student with a face-saving way out of the conflict; or using humor to defuse the confrontation (excerpted from Wright n.d., online).

Rhode, Jenson, and Reavis also remind teachers to look carefully at the ways in which they request compliance or reprimand students because "used incorrectly, arguing, excuses, tantrums, aggression, and noncompliance will increase" (1992, 58). They provide suggestions for teachers on ways to use requests for specific behavior or reprimands effectively:

- do not use a question format such as "Isn't it time to get your work started?" unless "no" is an acceptable answer;
- limit the space between you and the student or students to no more than three feet; in addition to taking advantage of proximity, this will decrease the likelihood that you will raise your voice;
- use a quiet voice;
- make eye contact;

Effective Classroom Management to Support Student Learning

> ### Dealing with Inappropriate Behavior—Two Tips
>
> - If the student argues with you when you assign a consequence, let him know that if he feels something is unfair he can make an appointment to talk to you about it at a later time. If he continues to argue, use the "broken record" technique—calmly restating the consequence and what the student should be doing. "The consequence for knocking Lou's book off the desk is owing one minute of recess, and now you need to take your seat and begin your math assignment."
>
> - Keep in mind that although consequences are necessary for aggressive acts, when they are implemented poorly they can backfire. If the consequence communicates the idea that adults are trying to use their power to "control" the student, there is a good chance that he will work hard to rebel and/or engage in power struggles. Thus, always use as mild a consequence as reasonably fits the infraction and be very calm in communicating the consequence to the student, avoid intensifying the consequence to "get back" at the student (Sprick and Howard 2004, online).

- provide time (five to 10 seconds) for the student to comply without interrupting by restating the request or by making a new request;

- ask no more than twice—and use preplanned consequences if the student does not comply;

- make only one request at a time; don't string requests together;

- describe the behavior that you want;

- be calm, not emotional—don't yell, threaten, or use deprecating statements; and

- verbally reinforce compliance (excerpted from 1992, 58-61).

Ineffective Disciplinary Practices

So far, the focus here has been on effective approaches to classroom management and discipline. Research and teacher experiences, however, have also identified some teacher responses that are typically ineffective:

- *Harsh reprimands, sarcasm, scolding and lecturing students about their misbehavior, and threats.*

- *Labeling a student on the basis of his/her misbehavior.* When communicating to a student that his or her behavior is not acceptable, make sure to label the behavior and not the student. For example, instead of saying "John, you are very disruptive!" say "John, your running around the room is very disruptive!"

- *Sending students to the principal's office for minor disruptions or infractions of rules.* This portrays the teacher as weak and unable to handle problems without the assistance of others. It also reinforces misbehavior by students who view "going to the principal's office" as a way to demonstrate to peers that they have more control than the teacher.

- *Assigning school work or writing as punishment.* This teaches students to associate academics with punishment.

- *Corporal punishment* (Hamby 1995; DiGiulio 1995).

"All discipline situations have three variables: the teacher, the problem student, and the rest of the class. Of these three variables, the one over which teachers have 100% control is themselves" (Tileston 2004, 20).

Finally, Tileston makes some additional recommendations for behaviors the teacher should not engage in when responding to student misbehavior:

- Do not lose your temper, even when students make comments about you or your classroom. Practice letting comments go in one ear and out the other.... If you take comments personally, the situation is much more likely to escalate.

- Do not make idle threats.... Even if you can carry out the threat, do not make it to the whole class—make it privately to the person(s) involved.

- Do not put names on the board or otherwise humiliate students.

- Do not ignore poor behavior. The class knows the behavior is inappropriate, and if you ignore it, the class will assume that behavior is not a priority with you.

- Never treat one student differently from another. Behavior management should be consistent and fair (excerpted from 2004, 34-35).

Working with Parents to Improve Student Behavior

It is sometimes productive to involve parents in the process of helping students improve their behavior. In addition to informing parents about behavior problems, the initial contact should stress the improvement of the student's opportunities for learning as a primary goal.

Parents can help to define reasonable, specific, and measurable goals for their children as well as consequences for meeting or failing to meet those goals. Moreover, working with parents may increase the consistency between home and school expectations. Curwin and Mendler (1988) outline a six-step process for working with parents to improve behavior:

- Meet with the parent(s). Both parents should be involved in the process if the student is from a two-parent home. In cases where a single parent is assisted in child rearing by a grandparent, other relative, etc., that person also should be involved in the process. It is important that parents and other primary caregivers understand the role they play in helping the student achieve the agreed-upon goals.

- Determine the behavior to be targeted for improvement.

- Set a goal related to the behavior that is measurable and can be reached in a reasonable period of time.

- Set rewards for achieving the goal, and consequences for failing to achieve the goal. Rewards might include special privileges, the opportunity to work on special projects, etc. Consequences would include a revised process for working toward the goal.

- Consider developing a written contract to formalize the process.

- Determine how the student's progress will be monitored and what kinds of follow-up activities will be necessary. Pick a time for a follow-up meeting.

Chapter 6

A Schoolwide Approach to Behavior Management and Discipline

While the primary focus of this *What We Know About* is the classroom, it is also clear that an effective schoolwide approach to discipline provides a strong foundation for teacher efforts at the classroom level. Focused, proactive, and consistent attention to discipline-related issues—across the school—can help to minimize the time teachers spend reacting to inappropriate student behavior and so provide more time for teaching and learning. According to Horner, Sugai, and Horner:

> Among the most compelling messages from current efforts to address disruptive behavior in schools is to be proactive. Schools that invest in building student competence, thereby preventing discipline problems, have documented up to 50 percent reductions in office discipline referrals. The goals of these efforts are threefold: 1) reduce the large number of minor behavioral offenses committed by students who are generally compliant; 2) identify clearly the relatively small number of students who are unaffected by general disciplinary practices and who require more targeted behavior supports; and 3) build a social culture among students where there is great clarity about what is appropriate and inappropriate (2000, 20).

"Research shows that the most effective schools are those with a well-ordered environment and high academic expectations" (Wong and Wong 1998, 143).

Rosenberg suggests that a schoolwide approach to discipline is more likely to be effective than the "piecemeal" approach used by many schools because it:

promotes consistency by positively recognizing appropriate behaviors and acting upon inappropriate behaviors . . . [and also] sets in motion a culture of recognition that reduces the risk of students slipping into situations where they misbehave to get attention (in Brownell and Walther-Thomas 1999, 109).

To be effective, schoolwide approaches need active participation by the entire teaching staff—which may require that classroom management procedures change in some classrooms. Thus, the most effective schoolwide approaches begin with conversations among teachers. In Remboldt's view:

> It is clear that an effective effort must be holistic and continuing—well organized, orderly, methodical, predictable—with all the parts working together. All school personnel must commit themselves to the effort and carry out their roles consistently (1998, 34).

As in the classroom, it is more effective to take a proactive approach to encouraging positive behavior than to merely address instances of misbehavior. An effective schoolwide approach to discipline is created first and foremost as a preventive measure—one intended to ensure the safety and sense of security of students and staff and so create an environment supportive of high levels of learning.

"Proactive, schoolwide approaches are considered the best practice in addressing the challenge of maintaining discipline" (White et al. 2001, 3).

Algozzine et al. (2000) describe what they term a "unified discipline" approach in which both expectations and responses to infractions are consistent across the school. In their view, it is particularly important for children who are more likely to exhibit challenging behaviors to experience the same rules of behavior in different classrooms, so that they "learn that what happens when they misbehave is procedural, not personal" (2000, 44). Students with emotional problems or those with some types of learning disabilities may respond particularly well to a schoolwide approach since consistency typically is more critical for them than for most other children. If there is a common understanding and application of rules from classroom to classroom, it makes it simpler for these students to internalize the expectations for behavior.

A Schoolwide Approach to Behavior Management and Discipline

In addition, students with behavior problems need positive role models, structure, and specific behavior plans based on natural consequences. They need to be taught new behaviors to replace the undesirable ones. Doing so takes teamwork, flexibility, and determination on the part of all school staff members (Van Dyke, Stallings, and Colley 1995; Whelan 1996)—and may be more likely to happen in a school that takes a schoolwide approach.

Finally, Patterson and Protheroe talk about some undesirable consequences of letting all teachers "do their own thing" in regard to developing and applying rules for student behavior:

> Often, individual teachers are left to develop their own rules and expectations without schoolwide guidance, which results in inconsistencies that students use to their advantage. Thus, instead of discipline being a shared responsibility, the principal is left to manage discipline problems and misbehavior (2000, 72-73).

Elements of an Effective Schoolwide Approach

It is important to understand, first of all, that an effective schoolwide approach to discipline requires more than a list of schoolwide rules. Fager and Boss provide some commonsense direction for educators considering strengthening a schoolwide approach to discipline:

> students need to perceive discipline as being fair, consistent, and clear. Disciplinary policies . . . need to be age-appropriate, clear, and repeatedly communicated to students and parents" (in Pacific Resources for Education and Learning 1999, online).

In addition, dealing with disruptive behavior "early, fairly, and effectively" is critical, say Fager and Boss (in Pacific Resources for Education and Learning 1999, online).

> **An effective schoolwide approach to discipline requires more than a list of schoolwide rules.**

Clearly stated expectations understood by everyone in the school community form a bedrock for schools dealing effectively with student behavior. The

Learning First Alliance (2001) suggests that simple messages, such as "Be respectful, be safe, be kind" or "Respect yourself, respect others, respect property," should be expectations explicitly underlying more detailed rules.

Research highlights the importance of developing rules and consequences consistent with a school's philosophy of education and learning goals—and doing this with the involvement of all members of the school community (Schimmel 1997; Gaustad 1992). Scott and Hunter provide reasons why this involvement is important:

> When schoolwide expectations, policy, and consequences are inconsistently applied across staff, they become ambiguous to students. And when students cannot predict the outcome of a given behavior, a significant number will act inappropriately. However, when the entire school staff is involved in determining and agreeing upon schoolwide expectations, policy, and consequences, staff consistency and resulting student success are far more likely (2001, 15).

Effective programs also recognize the need to plan ahead for a range of student behaviors. While many students come to school prepared to transition successfully from home life to the rules and routines of school, some students require more direct instruction on this element of school life (Warger, Eavy, and Associates for the U.S. Department of Education, Office of Special Education and Rehabilitation Services/Office of Special Education Programs 1999). In the view of the Learning First Alliance, these students often require special instruction, support, and supplemental services. Specifically, 15 percent of students come to school:

> able to fit in and succeed with modest additional assistance, such as conflict resolution or emotion-management training.... [while] 5 percent or so engage in severe and chronic problem behaviors and need more intensive and ongoing help, such as regular individual counseling or placement in alternative programs that provide greater supervision, structure, and support (2001, 14).

However, Gaustad reminds us that, while effective schoolwide approaches recognize that students have different levels of need for such special services:

> Effective discipline goes beyond finding solutions to help and remediate the "5 percent or so" [and goes on] to encourage responsible behavior and to provide all students with a satisfying school experience (1992, 1).

Researchers at six universities, in partnership with schools using a variety of school-based prevention practices, studied the programs and their effects over a six-year period. They consistently found one factor in schools successfully implementing a schoolwide approach:

> First and foremost, *administrators are key to making prevention work* [emphasis in the original]. Their role is twofold: providing an environment that fosters positive behavior and making available specialized support and services that can interrupt cycles of negative behavior.

These researchers also identified the three primary components of promising programs designed to decrease the likelihood of problematic student behavior:

- prevention in the classroom (positive behavior management, social skills instruction, and academic enrichment);

- schoolwide prevention (unified discipline approach, shared expectations for socially competent behavior, and academic enrichment); and

- school-family-community linkages (parent partnerships and community services) (Center for Effective Collaboration and Practice 1998).

Rosenberg and his colleagues have developed a comprehensive approach to schoolwide discipline that he calls the PAR (Prevention, Action, and Resolution) Model (see figure 3 on page 72). The model incorporates elements—such as consequences for rule compliance as well as noncompliance—that its developers feel are key to effective schoolwide approaches. Also embedded in the PAR Model is the element of crisis management and intervention, because having this component understood by all staff in the school can help foster consistent responses to more severe misbehavior (Rosenberg and Jackman n.d.).

Cotton has reviewed research about schools with effective approaches to discipline and has found they are characterized by:

- staff commitment in establishing and maintaining appropriate student behavior as an essential precondition of learning;

- high expectations for appropriate student behavior that staff members communicate and model;

- clear rules and procedures that are developed with input from students, are clearly specified, and are made known to everyone in the school;

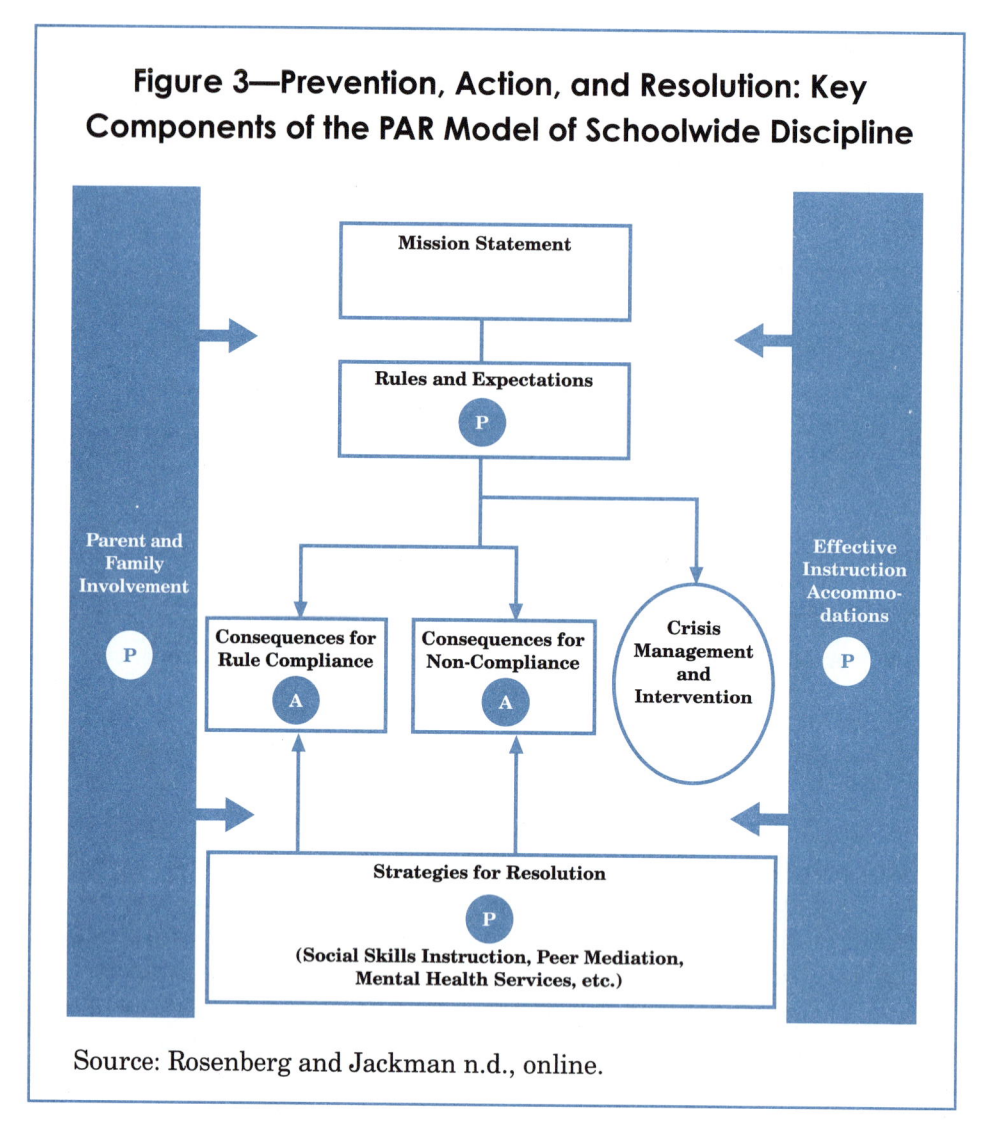

Figure 3—Prevention, Action, and Resolution: Key Components of the PAR Model of Schoolwide Discipline

```
                    Mission Statement
                           |
                  Rules and Expectations
                            (P)
          _____|_____
         |                   |                   |
  Consequences for    Consequences for        Crisis
  Rule Compliance     Non-Compliance       Management
        (A)                (A)           and Intervention
         |_____|_____|
                            |
                  Strategies for Resolution
                            (P)
           (Social Skills Instruction, Peer Mediation,
                  Mental Health Services, etc.)

  Parent and Family Involvement (P)    Effective Instruction Accommodations (P)
```

Source: Rosenberg and Jackman n.d., online.

- a principal who is visible in hallways and classrooms, talking informally with teachers and students, speaking to them by name, and expressing interest in their activities;

- teacher responsibility for handling routine classroom discipline problems, with support from the principal, who arranges for staff development on classroom management and discipline-related skills as needed; and

- close ties and a high level of communication with community members, who are kept abreast of the goings-on of the school through involvement in school functions and activities (2001, online).

A Schoolwide Approach to Behavior Management and Discipline

Finally, Kay and Ryan (2000) identify two additional teacher behaviors signaling classroom-based support for a schoolwide approach to discipline:

- embedding the teaching of social skills in their instruction; and
- encouraging suitable behavior by recognizing students when they behave appropriately.

Consistency Is Key

Wong and Wong make clear the degree to which an effective schoolwide approach must pervade the school and its practices, and highlight some of the features of consistent application:

- A schoolwide discipline plan is posted in every room, bus, office, gymnasium, cafeteria, library, hall, and other locations where there is an employee responsible for the safety and education of the students.
- The plan has the same basic design so that when a student goes from room to room or to the office, cafeteria, bus, library, or recess, it is the same basic plan.
- Since everyone at the school uses the same plan with consistency, the students know what is expected of them, and all members of the staff support one another. This also makes life much easier for new employees, because a plan is already in effect.
- Introducing a discipline plan to each new class of students is easy, because a plan, rooted in a prevailing culture, already exists at the school (1998, 144).

> "Consistency in the enforcement of what students should *not* do is not the only important aspect of a schoolwide discipline approach. It is equally important to acknowledge students who behave appropriately" (Brownell and Walther-Thomas 1999, 109).

Effective Classroom Management to Support Student Learning

> The *Improving the Lives of Children* project explicitly addresses some of the ways in which a school staff should embed consistency in its daily efforts to promote positive student behavior, including:
>
> - *Unified attitudes.* Teachers and other school personnel share the belief that instruction can improve behavior and that helping students develop positive behaviors is a legitimate part of teaching.
>
> - *Unified expectations.* Teachers and school personnel agree on expectations and consistently encourage them.
>
> - *Unified consequences.* When classroom and schoolwide rules are broken, teachers and school personnel respond in a consistent manner. Using a warm yet firm voice, they state the behavior, the violated rule, and the consequence.
>
> - *Unified team roles.* All personnel have clearly described responsibilities (Warger, Eavy, and Associates 1999, 9-10).

Developing a Schoolwide Discipline Plan

A needs assessment is an important first step when developing a schoolwide approach to discipline. For example, the staff might discuss behavior issues, determine where its collective strengths and weaknesses lie in terms of discipline, and explore how current policies help or harm the overall school climate. The principal can help to focus the discussion by asking probing questions such as "What are our problems?" and "Where do we go from here?"

Simply discussing these questions can help to increase understanding among staff members and so begin the move toward a more unified approach to discipline. For example, teachers with varying views on what constitutes a disruption in the hallways should attempt to come to a consensus on the elements of acceptable versus unacceptable behavior (Avellar-Fleming 1994).

Miles (1999) suggests that schools interested in revising their approach to discipline begin with a "behavior audit." Staff—and, in some instances, students and parents—are asked simple questions such as:

A Schoolwide Approach to Behavior Management and Discipline

- How do we believe students should behave in our school?
- What are some of our problems related to behavior?
- What do we currently do to help students behave appropriately?
- What are some ways we need to improve?

In his view, "the behavior audit is also a powerful exercise for students, and their beliefs about what is acceptable in a school will surprise most adults.... Students are also unbelievably accurate in their diagnosis of what works and what needs to be improved" (1999, 31).

Miles (1999) suggests that schools interested in revising their approach to discipline begin with a "behavior audit."

For example, one school asked: "If we were successful, what would our school be like?" After discussion, the staff established three goals to focus its efforts: "Students would solve their own problems in and out of the building, act appropriately, and show respect." To address the first goal, teachers were first "taught the language of problem solving" so that a common understanding of terms and procedures could be developed.

Students were taught to problem solve through very concrete interactions with staff who asked, for example, "What is the problem? What have you tried so far?" For the youngest children, pictures were used to help them understand and remember strategies such as an ice cube to symbolize cooling off. In the view of staff, these efforts eventually changed the culture of the school for the better (Littrell and Peterson 2001).

Reviewing data on past discipline problems can also be helpful. Specifically, are most of the problems occurring in the cafeteria, on the playground, or in particular hallways? Schools have also found that focusing on a few problems at first is often more effective and may also quickly improve the general atmosphere of the school.

One school identified a very specific goal—decreasing problems in the cafeteria. The staff decided to make a simple change in procedures: Students were no longer permitted to walk to a table at the front of the room to pick up

First Steps toward a Schoolwide Approach

Miles describes a process he has used with schools that have decided to implement a schoolwide approach:

> We begin by developing positively stated schoolwide rules and procedures. These can be adapted for unique situations and operationalized for the different developmental levels of students.... Specifically, we talk about reasonable rules versus unreasonable rules. The team develops procedures, such as taking students to the lunchroom, lavatory, late entry, etc. Usually, we address procedures that have been identified by the team as contributing to student behavior problems.... We also develop consequences for rule compliance, noncompliance, and procedures for crisis.
>
> We spend a significant amount of time developing consequences for compliance at the classroom level, team level, and schoolwide level, and mechanisms as to how these consequences are to be delivered. It is the team's expectation that all teachers and staff will deliver positive feedback for following school rules and procedures, such as coming prepared, using appropriate language, and following directions....[W]e encourage teams to think of ways to create a positive climate for students and faculty.
>
> It may be hard to believe, but establishing positive consequences is the most difficult part of the planning process, because many schools with high rates of behavior problems do not have a positive culture. Most often, educators tend to think of how we can punish bad behavior rather than promote appropriate behavior.
>
> One silver lining in this situation is that the team has an easier time in the next step of the process, developing consequences of noncompliance. The team develops a hierarchy of consequences so that students know what to expect if they break rules. Developing a hierarchy of consequences requires that the team think of systematic and fair consequences for inappropriate behavior. This way, teachers can avoid sending students to the office because they are "fed up" with their behavior, and administrators know that students were sent to the office for more serious behaviors and that they must respond consistently to those behaviors. Students do not get an office referral unless they have committed a certain offense.
>
> In implementing the system of consequences, we encourage school personnel to present the consequences as the products of choices the students make. Students know if they engage in appropriate behavior they can earn certain positive rewards. On the other hand, if students choose to act inappropriately, they know what the negative consequences are. This way, students can choose to

A Schoolwide Approach to Behavior Management and Discipline

> act appropriately or inappropriately. Helping students learn that consequences are the result of their behavior develops an internal locus of control that many students with cognitive and behavioral disabilities lack. Moreover, when teachers have a plan for dealing with behavior, they can move away from reactive responses to negative behavior and take a more proactive approach, reducing their stress (in Brownell and Walther-Thomas 1999, 110-111).

forks, napkins, etc., but, instead, raised their hands and received the needed items from a roving cafeteria aide. This one change quickly and significantly decreased instances of shoving and minor disagreements among students, and greatly improved both the atmosphere in the cafeteria and students' attention in classes immediately following lunch.

Avoiding the "Traps"

Developing an effective approach to schoolwide discipline is a complex process. Horner, Sugai, and Horner identify what they describe as "traps" around which educators need to navigate as they collaborate in school efforts to design an effective disciplinary system:

- Trap No. 1: *Getting tough is enough.* In reality, it is simply not enough to get tough, without a proactive system for teaching and supporting appropriate behavior.

- Trap No. 2: *Focusing on the difficult few.* Although an effective disciplinary system must address the small number of students who engage in chronic and intense disruptive behavior, procedures must be in place to build schoolwide social competence.

- Trap No. 3: *Looking for the quick fix.* Building effective schoolwide discipline takes time. A reasonable period to design and establish an effective disciplinary system is three to five years.

- Trap No. 4: *Finding one powerful trick.* Schoolwide discipline is not achieved through a single strategy. It must include components for defining and teaching behavioral expectations, rapid and low-effort support for students who continue to display disruptive behavior, and high-intensity support for students with high-intensity behavior problems.

- Trap No. 5: *Believing someone has the solution.* An effective system will be designed to meet a school's specific needs—identified through active self-assessment—and be continuously evaluated and changed to meet changing needs and goals.

- Trap No. 6: *Believing more is better.* Instead of accumulating more and sometimes inconsistent programs and approaches to deal with disciplinary problems, it is more effective to eliminate practices that are not working and very carefully match new practices to specific school needs (2000, 22-23).

Communicating the Plan

Rules and their consequences should be communicated to students and their families by means such as newsletters, student assemblies, and handbooks. Gaustad (1992) also suggests that periodically restating rules and expectations—for example, after the long winter break—can provide helpful reminders. To ensure students *understand* "expectations for behavior as well as the incentives and consequences associated with adherence to or violation of those expectations" (U.S. Office of Special Education Programs 2000, online), they should be provided with opportunities to discuss their understanding of them.

In addition, Lawrence and Olvey (1994) remind principals to set aside time to discuss the school discipline plan with teachers—and to explain it to new teachers as they join the staff. Although this seems like "just good common sense," they had worked with school staffs that did not completely understand the school's plan and so were enforcing rules inconsistently. Gaustad elaborates:

> a policy on paper is meaningless in itself. Ongoing administrative support, inservice training in new techniques, continued communication, and periodic evaluation and modification are needed to adapt a school discipline plan to the changing needs of the school community (1992, 3).

What Some Schools Have Done

When one Oregon elementary school sought to improve discipline, it adopted an approach called Effective Behavior Support. The staff credits its use of the Effective Behavior Support System for significantly decreasing discipline problems in the school. Elements included in the approach are:

- social skills training for students;
- academic restructuring, such as taking the first two days of an academic semester to orient new students to the code of conduct, give tours, and demonstrate acceptable behavior;
- flexibility with resources, such as reallocating funds and teacher's roles;
- behavioral interventions that address areas where students are having problems; and
- schoolwide goals, generally from three to five, that must be stated positively and have the consensus of staff members. The staff also demonstrates the goals and teaches students how to apply them. For example, "being responsible" could be translated into having children put their gym shoes away after class (Sack 2000, online).

In another example, Rudy Malesich, a middle school principal, describes his school's approach to discipline that, in one year, significantly decreased the number of referrals for intimidation or fighting. In his view, there are five simple keys to the success of the approach his school uses:

- Consistency—consequences are the same for everyone.
- Learning—students are encouraged to make good choices both in and out of school.
- Parents, students, and community members—they play an important part in initiating, implementing, and evaluating the program, and their involvement has fostered universal buy-in.
- Real-life consequences—law enforcement is involved both in and out of school.
- A focus on the problem of inappropriate choice, not on the students—students, parents, teachers, and administrators are constantly reminded that good students make bad choices and there are logical consequences for inappropriate choices in school as well as outside of school (1994, 39-40).

In one Oregon school, the faculty developed five goals, called "High Fives": Be respectful, be responsible, hands and feet to self, follow directions, and be there/be ready. Students who met the goals were rewarded with redeemable tickets for popcorn or extra time during lunch (Sack 2000, online).

The Making of Classroom Citizens: Consistency Management and Cooperative Discipline

The Consistency Management and Cooperative Discipline approach developed by Dr. Jerome Freiberg consists of two interrelated parts. First, Consistency Management, which is a philosophy and set of practices designed to create a supportive, but firm, and orderly classroom where familiar routines and quiet methods of communicating expectations to students replace chaotic and inconsistent attempts at control. The second part is Cooperative Discipline, which is a philosophy and set of practices designed to create experiences that develop students' self-discipline and participation in the life of the classroom.

The program has a high success rate because self-discipline replaces teacher-imposed discipline, allowing students to share in the responsibility for classroom management. For example, CMCD classrooms create as many as 50 "jobs" for students. Students "apply" for specific jobs, in writing, and are interviewed for them by their teacher. There is a substitute manager, a new-student welcomer, an attendance manager, and a student who passes out papers, among other positions. Jobs are rotated every four to six weeks so that all students hold positions in the classroom.

Dr. Kim Agnew, principal in a Texas elementary school using the approach, believes that teachers have regained valuable instructional time because they now share responsibility for daily classroom management tasks with students. "We estimate that we gain 25 to 30 minutes a day in instructional time," Agnew says. "Teachers have much more energy to put into planning lessons that engage their students, rather than constantly putting out fires."

Adds Agnew: "Our children thrive on order and routine. At home these things are lacking, so we need to give it to them. They line up quietly in the same place in line everyday; they just need to know what to expect. They look to us to provide this for them."

Creating ownership for classroom rules is essential if students are to become self-governing and if learning time is to be maximized, according to one teacher. "I've really been surprised by the level of ownership they take," she says. "I think it makes a difference that they've created the rules. Now it's not me saying 'Don't do that'; it's them saying, 'Hey, remember our rule.' "

Enforcement is done quietly, usually through an established system of nonverbal cues and hand gestures, like hand-raising. Each student also has a card on the blackboard for writing down an "infraction" when the teacher has to speak to him/her about classroom behavior.

A Schoolwide Approach to Behavior Management and Discipline

> Schools using CMCD develop strategies and practices designed to create consistent classroom environments with specific routines for such chaotic periods as the beginnings and endings of lessons and periods. Teachers are taught how to plan effective lessons that engage students and how to keep students flowing from one learning center to another to decrease boredom and idle hands. Such techniques help ensure an orderly classroom and help teachers get learning back on track (Porch and Protheroe 2002, 12-13).

Finally, Cotton cautions schools that, "if commercial, packaged discipline programs are used, modify their components to meet your unique school situation and delete those components which are not congruent with research" (2001, online).

The Role of the Principal

Development of an effective approach to managing student behavior requires planning, collaboration among staff members, efforts to educate students and staff about problems and possible solutions, attention to detail, and ongoing evaluation to identify what does or does not work. This complex task—only one among many important to the management of a good school—requires effective leadership. Horner, Sugai, and Horner talk about this:

> We know schoolwide discipline requires the sustained use of effective classroom and behavior management practices by teachers, staff members and families. However, we also know that workshops on classroom management procedures, anger management training and crisis management strategies will produce minimal effects without clear, consistent leadership. The building principal is the key person affecting establishment of schoolwide discipline (2000, 20).

Research and practice have consistently demonstrated that a school climate that conveys order, a sense of community, and higher expectations for behavior for both staff and students has a positive effect on student learning. As instructional leader in the school, the principal can be a strong force for creating this type environment. Gaustad sees the successful principal as a:

... highly visible model ... engaging in "management by walking around," greeting students and teachers, and informally monitoring possible problem areas.... Effective principals are liked and respected, rather than feared, and communicate caring for students as well as willingness to impose punishment if necessary (1992, 2).

Principals successful in addressing the need to foster high levels of appropriate student behavior understand that the task should be broadly defined—not limited to developing a list of rules and dealing with misbehavior. These leaders build a firm foundation for such a school by:

- *Cultivating an organizational structure that promotes values, beliefs, and rules that correspond with the school's goal, as stated in the discipline plan.* For example, the principal could promote the goal of increasing student involvement in school life by encouraging extracurricular activities, displaying student work in the hallways, or giving students a responsibility for maintaining the school grounds.

- *Communicating high expectations for students to both teachers and students.* In doing this, the principal helps to establish a climate in which students have high expectations for themselves, both academic and behavioral.

- *Being visible in classrooms and halls, and showing interest in everything that goes on at the school.*

- *Getting to know students as individuals* and *demonstrating an interest in their plans and activities.*

- *Encouraging teachers to handle all classroom discipline problems that they reasonably can and supporting their decisions.*

- *Providing opportunities for teachers to learn about effective management strategies and to work with fellow teachers to improve their management techniques.* Evidence shows that training teachers in effective management strategies can increase the use of key management principles and can heighten student task engagement. Beginning teachers are in particular need of training; classroom management is often cited as a major weakness of novice teachers, and stress related to classroom management is the most influential factor in failure among beginning teachers.

- *Supporting teachers in their daily work.* Principals can back up teachers in difficult situations where help is clearly necessary. Another way to express support is to let teachers know they will not be penalized for efforts that do not meet with success. For example, when implementing alternative task structures such as cooperative learning—which may result in a classroom that seems noisier or more disorderly than one in which a lecture-based approach is being used—teachers need reassurance that they will not automatically be perceived as lenient or disorganized. Blank and Kershaw write, "there must be an overall climate within schools that is supportive of risk taking" (1993, 12).

- *Working together with teachers and parents to help students assume responsibility for their actions.* In meetings with parents, administrators can work to develop an agreement on the basic expectations for behavior both in school and out of school, and how these behaviors might be taught to students.

- *Accepting responsibility for identifying and addressing problems that act as barriers to developing and maintaining an orderly school climate.*

- *Modeling prosocial behaviors—such as respecting others and working together to resolve conflicts—on a daily basis.* This is one of the most basic, yet most essential tasks of the principal (Cotton 2001; Drummond 1991; Evertson 1989; Greenlee and Ogletree 1993; Hartzell and Petrie 1992).

Chapter 7

Concluding Remarks

Each chapter of this *What We Know About* highlights the importance of teacher knowledge and skills to the aspect of teaching known as classroom management. Fundamentally, classroom management is about providing an environment in which students can learn. Although this goal is basic, the strategies necessary for effective management are varied and extend across a variety of classroom and school situations. Effective classroom management is a complex task.

For example, in order to manage classrooms well, teachers must be knowledgeable about and skillful in the following:

- developing a system of rules and consequences appropriate for the developmental level of the students in the classroom;
- setting up the physical environment in ways that minimize disruptions and maximize opportunities for learning;
- helping students learn how to gain control over their own behavior; and
- responding to misbehavior.

It is also important to recognize that teachers are continuously "on stage." Their daily actions—no matter how small—are constantly providing lessons for students. However, ensuring that the lessons are always positive ones is sometimes easier said than done. For example, each of us can imagine the growing frustration of a teacher whose students just can't seem to settle down. A very natural reaction might be to slap books on a desk and use a loud and angry voice to ask, "Why are you all being so stupid this morning?" This might be an effective way—at least in the short term—to grab students' attention. But the messages embedded in it—that it is appropriate to lose one's temper and to use name calling to make a point—are not good lessons.

Now mentally compare that lesson to the message sent by an alternative approach. Clearly and calmly, the teacher might say:

> I felt angry this morning when you all misbehaved during the math lesson. By talking to your neighbors instead of paying attention to me, you did not show me respect. Just as important, you missed some important points in the lesson. Let's start over—but this time I want to see good behavior that makes it easier for all of us to do our jobs.

This approach makes clear what caused the teacher to become angry, does it in a way that does not demonstrate disrespect to the students, and establishes the expectation that the students can behave appropriately. Every teacher has dozens of opportunities for lessons such as these every week. The challenge is becoming so well prepared that using an effective approach becomes second nature.

The discussion would be incomplete without mentioning the key role teacher attitudes play in setting a tone for the classroom. In an interview, the late Fred Rogers, of "Mr. Rogers" fame, talked about this:

> An old Quaker adage says, "Attitudes are caught, not taught." The teacher sets the attitude of the classroom—and that attitude is contagious. Children learn from their teacher's example, from the way the teacher respects each child and from the way the teacher expects children to treat one another (Starr 2002, online).

Palardy talks about some specific aspects of teacher attitudes that are just as important as more concrete aspects of classroom management such as rules and consequences. He suggests each teacher should strive to:

- Feel comfortable with yourself, your students, and what you are teaching. Any uneasiness is quickly communicated to students and can cause bad behavior.

- Believe in your students' ability to behave. Such beliefs are self-fulfilling prophesies: students tend to misbehave if their teacher believes that they can't or won't act appropriately.

- Remember that students are not adults. Children should not be expected to control their behavior to the extent that adults can.

- *Show that you genuinely respect your students.* Earning your students' respect is probably the most important strategy of all in promoting positive behavior (1993, 1-2).

Effective classroom management is proactive, accentuates the positive, provides opportunities for students to develop their own self-management skills, and is an integral aspect of the classroom environment. The task also is much broader than simply dealing with misbehavior. It involves creating and maintaining a delicate balance of control, while not stifling students' energy and creativity.

Finally, it requires an understanding of the relationship between classroom management and instruction. It simply is easier for students to focus on learning in a classroom in which misbehavior is the exception, not the rule. And students are more likely to behave appropriately when instruction is engaging and geared to their individual abilities and needs.

While "good classroom management is almost invisible" (Freiberg 2002, 56), its impact can be substantial in terms of student learning. Good classroom management makes good instruction possible.

References

Abramowitz, A.J., O'Leary, S.G., & Futtersak, M.W. (1988). The relative impact of long and short reprimands on children's off-task behavior in the classroom. *Behavior Therapy, 18*, 243-247.

Abrams, B.J., & Segal, A. (1998). How to prevent aggressive behavior. *Teaching Exceptional Children* (March/April 1998), 10-15.

Alber, S., & Heward, W. (1996). 'Gotcha!' Twenty-five behavior traps guaranteed to extend your students' academic and social skills. *Intervention in School and Clinic* (May 1996), 285-289.

Algozzine, B., Audette, B., Ellis, E., Marr, M.B., & White, R. (2000). Supporting teachers, principals—and students—through unified discipline. *Teaching Exceptional Children* (November/December 2000), 42-47.

American Federation of Teachers. (n.d.). *Setting the stage for high standards: Elements of effective school discipline.* Washington, DC: Author. Retrieved from http://www.aft.org/edissues/elements/Eleone.htm

Arnold, J.B., & Dodge, H.W. (1994). Room for all. *The American School Board Journal, 181*(10), 22-26.

Avellar-Fleming, C. (1994). Seven steps to discipline. *The Executive Educator* (November 1994), 32-34.

Bae, S. (2002). Using functional assessments to develop effective behavioral interventions. *Reclaiming Children and Youth* (Winter 2002), 213-215.

Bicard, D.F. (2000). Using classroom rules to construct behavior. *Middle School Journal* (May 2000), 37-38.

Black, S. (2003). Angry at the world. *American School Board Journal* (June 2003), 43-45.

Blank, M.A., & Kershaw, C. (1993, April). *Perceptions of educators about classroom management demands when using interactive strategies.* Paper presented at the annual meeting of the American Educational Research Association, Atlanta, GA. (ERIC Document Reproduction Service Number 358137)

Bodine, R.K., & Crawford, D.K. (1998). *The handbook of conflict resolution education: A guide to building quality programs in schools.* San Francisco: Jossey-Bass.

Booth, R.C. (n.d.). *List of appropriate school-based accommodations and interventions.* Pottstown, PA: Attention Deficit Disorder Association. Retrieved from http://www.add.org/content/school/list.htm

Brandt, R. (1990). On learning styles: A conversation with Pat Guild. *Educational Leadership, 48*(2), 10-13.

Brock, S. (2000). Helping the student with ADHD in the classroom: Strategies for teachers. *Communique* (Spring 2000), 18-20.

Brophy, J. (n.d.). *Teaching.* Geneva, Switzerland: International Academy of Education. Retrieved from http://www.ibe.unesco.org

Brophy, J., & Good, T. (1986). Teacher behavior and student achievement. In M.C. Wittrock (Ed.), *Handbook of Research on Teaching, Third Edition.* New York: Macmillan Publishing Company.

Brownell, M.T., & Walther-Thomas, C. (1999). An interview with Dr. Michael Rosenberg: Preventing school discipline problems schoolwide. *Intervention in School & Clinic* (November 1999), 108-112.

Buck, G.H. (1992). Classroom management and the disruptive child. *Music Educators Journal, 79*(3), 36-42.

Burnett, E.M.G. (2000). Conflict resolution: Four steps worth taking. *Social Studies and the Young Learner* (January/February 2000), 20-23.

Carlson, P.M., & Peterson, R.L. (1995). Changing behavior with humor. *Reclaiming Children and Youth 4*(2), 28-30.

Carter, J.E. (1993). Self-management: Education's ultimate goal. *Teaching Exceptional Children, 25*(3), 28-32.

Center for Effective Collaboration and Practice. (1998). *Prevention strategies that work: What administrators can do to promote positive student behavior.* Washington, DC: Author. Retrieved from http://cecp.air.org/preventionstrategies/prevent.pdf

Center for Effective Collaboration and Practice. (2000). *Functional behavior assessment.* Retrieved from: http://cecp.air.org/fba/default.htm

Churchward, B. (n.d.). 11 techniques for better classroom discipline. Retrieved from http://www.honorlevel.com/techniques.html

Cohen, E.G. (1991, April). *Classroom management and complex instruction.* Paper presented at the annual meeting of the American Educational Research Association, Chicago, IL. (ERIC Document Reproduction Number 333547)

Collaborative for Excellence in Teacher Preparation. (n.d.). *Temple teachers' connection.* Retrieved from http://www.temple.edu/CETP/temple_teach/cm-routi.html

Cotton, K. (2001). Schoolwide and classroom discipline. *School Improvement Research Series.* Retrieved from http://www.nwrel.org/scpd/sirs/5/cu9.html

Curwin, R.L., & Mendler, A.N. (1988). *Discipline with dignity.* Alexandria, VA: Association for Supervision and Curriculum Development.

DiGiulio, R. (1995). *Positive classroom management.* Thousand Oaks, CA: Corwin Press, Inc.

Drummond, R.J. (1991). *How principals rate beginning teachers.* Washington, DC: National Council for Accreditation of Teacher Education. (ERIC Document Reproduction Service Number 341657)

Eisler, J.A., Lane, P., & Mei. L. (1995). A comprehensive conflict resolution training program. *ERS Spectrum, 13*(1), 25-33.

Erk, R.R. (1999). Attention deficit hyperactivity disorder: Counselors, laws, and implications for practice. *Professional Counseling* (April 1999), 318-326.

Evertson, C.M. (1989). Improving elementary classroom management: A school-based training program for beginning the year. *Journal of Educational Research, 83*(2), 82-90.

Foster, S.L., Brennan, P., Biglan, A., Wang, L., & al-Ghaith, S. (2002). *Preventing behaviour problems: What works.* Brussels, Belgium: The International Academy of Education.

Freiberg, H.J. (2002). Essential skills for new teachers. *Educational Leadership* (March 2002), 56-60.

Fuhr, D. (1993). Effective classroom discipline: Advice for educators. *NASSP Bulletin* (January 1993), 83-86.

Gaustad, J. (1992). *School discipline* (ERIC Digest). Eugene, OR: ERIC Clearinghouse on Educational Management. (ED 350727).

Gay, G. (2000). *Improving the achievement of marginalized students of color.* Aurora, CO: Mid-Continent Research for Education and Learning.

Good, T.L. (1987). Two decades of research on teacher expectations: Findings and future directions. *Journal of Teacher Education, 38*(4), 32-47.

Gottfredson, D.C., et al. (1995). Increasing teacher expectations for student achievement. *Journal of Educational Research* (January/February 1995), 155-163.

Greenberg, P. (1992). Ideas that work with young children: How to institute some simple democratic practices pertaining to respect, rights, roots, and responsibilities in any classroom (without losing your leadership position). *Young Children* (July 1992), 10-17.

References

Greenlee, A.R., & Ogletree, E.J. (1993). *Teachers' attitudes toward student discipline problems and classroom management strategies*. Chicago: Chicago Public Schools. (ERIC Document Reproduction Service Number 364330).

Gunter, P.L., Jack, S.L., Depaepe, P., Reed, T.M., & Harrison, J. (1994). Effects of challenging behaviors of students with EBD on teacher instructional behavior. *Preventing School Failure* (Spring 1994), 35-39.

Haberman, M. (1995). *Star teachers of children in poverty*. West Lafayette, IN: Kappa Delta Pi.

Hall, P.S., & Hall, N.D. (2003). Building relationships with challenging children. *Educational Leadership* (September 2003), 60-63.

Hamby, J.V. (1995). *Straight talk about discipline*. Clemson, SC: National Dropout Prevention Center.

Hartzell, G.N., & Petrie, T.A. (1992). The principal and discipline: Working with school structures, teachers, and students. *The Clearing House, 65*(6), 376-380.

Hendra, M. (2004, October 12). Time on the sofa for good behavior. *The Christian Science Monitor*. Retrieved from http://www.csmonitor.com/2004/1012/p13s01-cogn.html

Hewitt, M.B. (1999). The control game: Exploring oppositional behavior. *Reclaiming Children and Youth* (Spring 1999), 30-33.

Horner, R.H., Sugai, G., & Horner, H.F. (2000). A schoolwide approach to student discipline. *The School Administrator* (February 2000), 20-23.

Horsch, P., Chen, J., & Nelson, D. (1999). Rules and rituals: Tools for creating a respectful, caring learning community. *Phi Delta Kappan* (November 1999), 223-227.

Ikram, M., & Bratlien, M.J. (1994). Better disciplined schools: Is mediation the answer? *NASSP Bulletin, 78*(562), 43-50.

Johnson, D.W., & Johnson, R.T. (1995). Why violence prevention programs don't work—and what does. *Educational Leadership* (February 1995), 63-67.

Johnson, D.W., Johnson, R.T., Dudley, B., & Burnett, R. (1992). Teaching students to be peer mediators. *Educational Leadership, 50*(1), 10-13.

Johnson, L.M., & Protheroe, N. (2003). *What we know about: Culture and learning*. Arlington, VA: Educational Research Service.

Johnson, L.R., & Johnson, C.E. (1999). Teaching students to regulate their own behavior. *Teaching Exceptional Children* (March/April 1999), 6-10.

Jones, F.H. (1987). *Positive classroom discipline*. New York: McGraw-Hill.

Kay, P., & Ryan, K. (2000). Prevention strategies for the elementary school classroom. *Behavioral Interventions: Creating a Safe Environment in Our Schools* (Winter 2000). Retrieved from http://www.naspcenter.org/pdf/BehInt2k.pdf

Knapp, M.S., Shields, P.M., & Turnbull, B.J. (1992). *Academic challenge for the challenge of poverty: Summary report*. Washington, DC: U.S. Department of Education, Office of Policy and Planning.

Kohn, A. (1993). Choices for children: Why and how to let students decide. *Phi Delta Kappan, 75*(1), 8-16,18-21.

Kottler, J.A. (2002). *Students who drive you crazy: Succeeding with resistant, unmotivated, and otherwise difficult young people*. Thousand Oaks, CA: Corwin Press, Inc.

Landau, B.M., & Gathercoal, P. (2000). Creating peaceful classrooms: Judicious discipline and class meetings. *Phi Delta Kappan* (February 2000), 450-454.

Lane, P.S., & McWhirter, J.J. (1992). A peer mediation model: Conflict resolution for elementary and middle school children. *Elementary School Guidance & Counseling, 27*(1), 15-23.

Latham, A.S. (1998). Research link: Rules and learning. *Educational Leadership*. (September 1998). Retrieved from http://www.ascd.org.safeschools/e19809/sellatham.html

Lawrence, P.A., & Olvey, S.K. (1994). Discipline: A skill not a punishment. *The American School Board Journal, 181*(7), 31-32.

Learning First Alliance. (2001). *Every child learning: Safe and supportive schools.* Baltimore: Author.

Lein, L., Johnson, J.F., & Ragland, M. (1997). *Successful Texas schoolwide programs: Research study results.* Austin, TX: The Charles Dana Center.

Lindberg, J.A., Kelley, D.E., & Swick, A.M. (2005). *Common-sense classroom management for middle and high school teachers.* Thousand Oaks, CA: Corwin Press.

Littrell, J.M., & Peterson, J.S. (2001). Transforming the school culture: A model based on an exemplary counselor. *Professional School Counseling* (June 2001), 310-319.

Lumsden, L. (1997). Expectations for students. *ERIC Digest No.116*, Eugene, OR: ERIC Clearinghouse on Educational Management.

Malesich, R.F. (1994). Making schools safe for students. *Schools in the middle* (February 1994), 38-40.

Marzano, R.J. (2003). *What works in schools: Translating research into action.* Alexandria, VA: Association for Supervision and Curriculum Development.

Marzano, R.J., & Marzano, J.S. (2003). The key to classroom management. *Educational Leadership* (September 2003), 6-13. Retrieved from http://www.ascd.org/publications/ed_lead/200309/marzano.html

Marzano, R.J., Marzano, J.S., & Pickering, D.J. (2003). *Classroom management that works: Research-based strategies for every teacher.* Alexandria, VA: Association for Supervision and Curriculum Development.

McLeod, J., Fisher, J., & Hoover, G. (2003). *The key elements of classroom management: Managing time and space, student behavior, and instructional strategies.* Alexandria, VA: Association for Supervision and Curriculum Development.

Miles, B.H. (1999). Getting everybody on the same page: Conducting a behavior audit. *The High School Magazine* (May/June 1999), 30-32.

Mills, D., & Bulach, C. (1996, March). *Behavior disordered students in collaborative/cooperative classes: Does behavior improve?* Paper presented at the annual meeting of the National Dropout Prevention Conference, Tampa, FL.

Morrow, L.M., Tracey, D., Woo, D., & Pressley, M. (1999). Characteristics of exemplary first-grade literacy instruction. *The Reading Teacher* (February 1999), 462-476.

Nichtor, M. (2002). Families that fight. *ASCA School Counselor* (September-October 2002), 24-27.

O'Neil, J. (1990). Making sense of style. *Educational Leadership, 48*(2), 4-9.

O'Neil, J. (2004). Classroom management: Discipline zingers. *NEA Today* (January 2004), 24-33.

Pacific Resources for Education and Learning. (1999). *Focused discussion ... peaceful schools.* Honolulu, HI: Author.

Palardy, J.M. (1993). Classroom discipline: The diagnostic approach. *NAESP Streamlined Seminar* (June 1993), 1-4.

Patterson, J., & Protheroe, N. (2000). *Essentials for principals: A school leader's guide to special education.* Alexandria, VA: National Association of Elementary School Principals and Arlington, VA: Educational Research Service.

Petrie, G., Lindauer, P., Bennett, B., & Gibson, S. (1998). Nonverbal cues: The key to classroom management. *Principal* (January 1998), 34-36.

Porch, S., & Protheroe, N. (2002). Classroom management. *ERS Focus On*, 1-16.

Prater, M.A. (1994). Improving academic and behavior skills through self-management procedures. *Preventing School Failure, 38*(4), 5-9.

Public Agenda. (2004). *Teaching interrupted: Do discipline policies in today's public schools foster the common good?* New York: Author. Retrieved from http://www.publicagenda.org/research/pdfs/teaching_interrupted.pdf

References

Rademacher, J.A., Callahan, K., & Pederson-Seelye, V.A. (1998). How do your classroom rules measure up? Guidelines for developing an effective rule management routine. *Intervention in School and Clinic* (May 1998), 284-289.

Reed, D.F. (1991). Effective classroom managers in the middle school. *Middle School Journal* (September 1991), 16-21.

Remboldt, C. (1998). Making violence unacceptable. *Educational Leadership* (September 1998), 32-38.

Rhode, G., Jenson, W.R., & Reavis, H.K. (1992). *The tough kid book: Practical classroom management strategies*. Longmont, CO: Sopris West.

Rosenberg, M., & Jackman, L. (n.d.). *Up to PAR: Successful implementation and maintenance of comprehensive school-wide discipline programs*. Baltimore: Johns Hopkins University. Retrieved from http:// www.parproject.org/manuals/acrobat/Par_infoPack.pdf

Sack, J. (2000). Oh, behave. *Teacher Magazine*. (January 2000). Retrieved from http:// www.teachermagazine.org/tm/tmstory.cfm.h11

Schimmel, D. (1997). Traditional rule-making and the subversion of citizenship education. *Social Education* (February 1997), 70-74.

Scott, T., & Hunter, J. (2001). Initiating schoolwide support systems: An administrator's guide to the process. *Beyond Behavior* (Fall 2001), 13-15.

Seeman, H. (1988). *Preventing classroom discipline problems: A guide for educators*. Lancaster, PA: Technomic Publishing Co., Inc.

Shandler, N. (1996). Just rewards. *Teaching Tolerance* (Spring 1996). Retrieved from http:// www.tolerance.org/teach/expand/mag/features.jsp?p=0&is=10&ar=63

Shapiro, E.S., & Cole, C.L. (1994). *Behavior change in the classroom: Self-management interventions*. New York: The Guilford Press.

Shaughnessy, J.G., Coughlin, M., & Smith, K. (1997). Dealing with disruptive behaviors in high school classrooms. *The High School Magazine* (June/July 1997), 44-47.

Shockley, R., & Sevier, L. (1991). Behavior management in the classroom: Guidelines for maintaining control. *Schools in the Middle* (Winter 1991), 14-18.

Shore, R.E., Gunter, P.L., & Jack, S.L. (1993). Classroom management strategies: Are they setting events for coercion? *Behavioral Disorders, 18,* 92-102.

Sileo, T.W., & Prater, M.A. (1998). Creating classroom environments that address the linguistic and cultural backgrounds of students with disabilities: An Asian Pacific American perspective. *Remedial and Special Education* (November/December 1998), 323-337.

Smith, M.A., & Misra, A. (1992). A comprehensive management system for students in regular classrooms. *The Elementary School Journal* (July 1992), 362-364.

Sousa, D.A. (2003). *How the gifted brain learns*. Thousand Oaks, CA: Corwin Press.

Sprick, R.S., & Howard, L.M. (2004). *The teacher's encyclopedia of behavior management*. Longmont, CO: Sopris West. Retrieved from http://www.state.ky.us/agencies/behave/bi/encyagg/aggress2.html

Starr, L. (2002). Mister Rogers reflects on respect, diversity, and the classroom neighborhood. *Education World* (October 14, 2002). Retrieved from http://www.educationworld.com/a_curr/profdev016.shtml

Stewart, S.C., Evans, W.H., & Kaczynski, D.J. (1997). Setting the stage for success: Assessing the instructional environment. *Preventing School Failure* (Winter 1997), 53-56.

Strauss, V. (2002, November 11). Short attention span theater: Educators at all levels mix activities into classroom discussions to keep students focused on subject at hand. *The Washington Post*. Retrieved online at www.washingtonpost.com/wp-dyn/articles/A7446-2002Nov18.html

Sumpter, R.D., & Kidd, L. (Fall 1998). ADD: How does it add up in the classroom? *Rural Educator, 20*(1), 12-15.

Tanner, B.M., Bottoms, G., Feagin, C., & Bearman, A. (1999). *Instructional strategies: How teachers teach matters*. Atlanta, GA: Southern Regional Education Board.

Taylor, B.M., Pearson, P.D., Clark, K., & Walpole, S. (1999). *Beating the odds in teaching all children to read*. Ann Arbor, MI: Center for the Improvement of Early Reading Achievement.

Teaching Today. (n.d.). *Establishing classroom rules*. Retrieved from http://www.glencoe.com/sec/teachingtoday/weeklytips.phtml/print/110

Tileston, D.W. (2004). *What every teacher should know about classroom management and discipline*. Thousand Oaks, CA: Corwin Press.

U.S. Office of Special Education Programs. (2000). *Schoolwide approaches to behavior*. Washington, DC: U.S. Department of Education, Office of Special Education Programs. Retrieved from http://www.ideapractices.org/docs/OSEPdocs/schoolwideapproach.htm

Van Dyke, R., Stallings, M.A., & Colley, K. (1995). How to build an inclusive school community: A success story. *Phi Delta Kappan* (February 1995), 475-480.

Vuko, E.P. (2003, November 25). Calming disruptive students. *The Washington Post*, p. C9.

Walberg, H.J., & Paik, S.J. (2004). Effective general practices. In Gordon Cawelti (Ed.), *Handbook of Research on Improving Student Achievement (Third Edition)*, pp. 25-38. Arlington, VA: Educational Research Service.

Walker, H.M., Colvin, G., & Ramsey, E. (1995). *Antisocial behavior in school: Strategies and best practices*. Pacific Grove, CA: Brooks/Cole Publishing Company.

Wall, A. (1993). How teacher location in the classroom can improve students' behavior. *The Clearing House, 66*(5), 299-301.

Wang, M.C., Haertel, G.D., & Walberg, H.J. (1993/1994). What helps students learn? *Educational Leadership*, (December 1993, January 1994), 74-79.

Warger, Eavy, and Associates for the U.S. Department of Education, Office of Special Education and Rehabilitation Services/Office of Special Education Programs. (1999). *Prevention strategies that work*. Burlington, VT: University of Vermont.

Weinstein, C., Curran, M., & Tomlinson-Clarke, S. (2003). Culturally responsive classroom management: Awareness into action. *Theory into Practice*. Retrieved from http://www.findarticles.com/p/articles/mi_m0NQM/is_4_42/ai_111506822

Wharton-McDonald, R., Pressley, M., & Hampston, J.M. (1998). Literacy instruction in nine first-grade classrooms: Teacher characteristics and student achievement. *The Elementary School Journal* (November 1998), 101-128.

Whelan, R.J. (1996). Classroom management. In E.L. Meyen, G.A. Vergason, and R.J. Whelan (Eds.), *Strategies for teaching exceptional children in inclusive settings*, pp. 303-310. Denver, CO: Love.

White, R., Algozzine, B., Audette, R., Marr, M.B, & Ellis Jr., E.D. (2001). Unified discipline: A school-wide approach for managing problem behavior. *Intervention in School and Clinic* (September 2001), 3-8.

Willis, S. (1996). Managing today's classroom: Finding alternatives to control and compliance. *ASCD Education Update* (September 1996), 1-7.

Wilson, E. (1996). *What we know about: Classroom management to encourage motivation and responsibility*. Arlington, VA: Educational Research Service.

Wise, B.J. (2003). Meaningful work motivates. *Leadership Compass* (Fall 2003), 1-3.

Wong, H.K., & Wong, R.T. (1998). *The first days of school*. Mountain View, CA: Harry K. Wong Publications, Inc.

Wright, J. (n.d.). *Dodging the power-struggle trap: Ideas for teachers*. Retrieved from http://www.interventioncentral.org/htmdocs

ORDER FORM FOR RELATED RESOURCES

		Price Per Item			
Quantity	Item # and Title	Base Price	ERS Individual Subscriber Discount Price	ERS School District Subscriber Discount Price	Total Price
	What We Know About: Effective Classroom Management to Support Student Learning (#0628)	$22	$16.50	$11	
	What We Know About: Building Classroom Community to Support Student Learning (#0629)	$22	$16.50	$11	
Single Copy Only	*Positive Discipline/Positive Reinforcement* (#5184)	$40	$30	$20	
Single Copy Only	*Caring School Environments* (#5303)	$40	$30	$20	

Postage and Handling ** (Add the greater of $4.50 or 10% of purchase price.):	
Express Delivery ** (Add $20 for second-business-day service.):	
TOTAL DUE:	

** Please double for international orders.

SATISFACTION GUARANTEED!
If you are not satisfied with an ERS resource, return it in its original condition within 30 days of receipt and we will give you a full refund.

Method of payment:

☐ Check enclosed (payable to Educational Research Service).

☐ Purchase order enclosed (P.O.#_____).

Bill my: ☐ VISA ☐ MasterCard ☐ American Express

Name on Card (print) _____

Account Number _____ Expiration Date _____

Signature _____ Date _____

Visit us online at www.ers.org for a complete listing of resources!

Shipping address:

☐ Dr. ☐ Mr. ☐ Mrs. ☐ Ms.   Name _____

Position _____ ERS Subscriber ID# _____

School District or Agency _____

Street Address _____

City _____ State _____ Zip _____

Phone _____ Fax _____ Email _____

Return completed order form to: Educational Research Service
2000 Clarendon Boulevard, Arlington, VA 22201-2908
Phone: (800) 791-9308 • Fax: (800) 791-9309 • Email: ers@ers.org • Web site: www.ers.org

ERS *Subscriptions at a Glance*

If you are looking for reliable K-12 research to . . .
- identify research-based teaching practices;
- make educationally sound and cost-effective decisions; and most importantly
- improve student achievement . . .

then you need look no further than an ERS Subscription.

Simply choose the subscription option that best meets your needs:

✓ **School District Subscription**—a special research and information subscription that provides education leaders with timely research on priority issues in K-12 education. All new ERS publications and periodicals, access to customized information services through the ERS special library, and 50 percent discounts on additional ERS resources are included in this subscription for one annual fee. This subscription also provides the entire administrative staff "instant" online, searchable access to the wide variety of ERS resources. You'll gain access to the ERS electronic library of more than 1,600 educational research-based documents, as well as additional content uploaded throughout the year.

✓ **Individual Subscription**—designed primarily for school administrators, staff, and school board members who want to receive a personal copy of new ERS studies, reports, and/or periodicals published and special discounts on other resources purchased.

✓ **Other Education Agency Subscription**—available for state associations, libraries, departments of education, service centers, and other organizations needing access to quality research and information resources and services.

Your ERS Subscription benefits begin as soon as your order is received and continue for 12 months. For more detailed subscription information and pricing, contact ERS toll free at (800) 791-9308, by email at ers@ers.org, or visit us online at www.ers.org!